To Do List

Reduces Stress and Increases Productivity

(An Easy to Use to Do List Formula to Save Hours of Your Time)

Steven Rouse

Published By **Zoe Lawson**

Steven Rouse

All Rights Reserved

To Do List: Reduces Stress and Increases Productivity (An Easy to Use to Do List Formula to Save Hours of Your Time)

ISBN 978-1-77485-974-2

No part of this guidebook shall be reproduced in any form without permission in writing from the publisher except in the case of brief quotations embodied in critical articles or reviews.

Legal & Disclaimer

The information contained in this ebook is not designed to replace or take the place of any form of medicine or professional medical advice. The information in this ebook has been provided for educational & entertainment purposes only.

The information contained in this book has been compiled from sources deemed reliable, and it is accurate to the best of the Author's knowledge; however, the Author cannot guarantee its accuracy and validity and cannot be held liable for any errors or omissions. Changes are periodically made to this book. You must consult your doctor or get professional medical advice before using any of the suggested remedies, techniques, or information in this book.

Upon using the information contained in this book, you agree to hold harmless the Author from and against any damages, costs, and expenses, including any legal fees potentially resulting from the application of any of the information provided by this guide. This disclaimer applies to any damages or injury caused by the use and application, whether directly or indirectly, of any advice or information presented, whether for breach of contract, tort, negligence, personal injury, criminal intent, or under any other cause of action.

You agree to accept all risks of using the information presented inside this book. You need to consult a professional medical practitioner in order to ensure you are both able and healthy enough to participate in this program.

Table of contents

Chapter 1: Own Your Time 1

Chapter 2: Neuroscience Behind To-Do Lists 13

Chapter 3: Why Did Your To Do List Fail? 21

Chapter 4: Composition Of Perfect Productivity 29

Chapter 5: Top 10 Task Management Systems 35

Chapter 6: How To Balance Work And Life 58

Chapter 7: Formulation Your Perfect To Do List 68

Chapter 8: Top 6 Productivity Enhancer Tips 84

Chapter 9: Pen-&-Paper Versus Digital List 92

Chapter 1: Own Your Time

"Let your advance worrying turn into advance thinking and planning." Winston Churchill

I was looking online for good bedtime stories for my son and found this one on the importance time. Even though it was a short story, it made me wonder long after my son fell asleep. It seems like the inexhaustible nature of the resource (i.e. time) should be ingrained into our children from childhood. To prepare them in a magical, even more beautiful future.

It was a story about Harry, a boy who used to spend his entire time in front the television. His parents wanted him play, to study, and to follow certain hobbies. However, he never paid any attention.

One fine day they went hiking. Harry sat down and took a rest. The next thing he knew, the rest of his group had disappeared. He was about ready to leave and go looking for others, when he saw the dwarf come out of the trees. He seemed angry, grumbling under his teeth, and moaning about something. All his anger caused him to be unaware that a boulder was rolling towards him. Harry saw it and jumped in, saving the dwarf. Without Harry's help, he would have been crushed underneath this boulder.

The dwarf was amazed but so grateful that Harry took him along to show Harry a secret place of the Dwarves. Both men walked through the Mountain until they reached a small clearing. A well appeared to be ordinary in the middle.

Dwarf declared enthusiastically, "It's a magic spring."

Harry didn't know whether to believe him.

"This is our source of unending wonders," said the dwarf.

He explained that magical gifts are often given out of the magical water and that everyone who is present can now enjoy them.

Harry looked at his dwarf, not certain if it was true or false. Then, he was shocked to see the incredible cycle that emerged from the well. Harry was thrilled and couldn't believe what he saw. He wanted to verify that it was not a trick, so he thoroughly examined the bicycle. When he was satisfied, he was about ready to ride the bicycle. Harry fell on the ground. Harry was mad, thinking the dwarf was trying to trick him and would have said some words. However, he was stunned when he saw another great gift. It was the coolest dress that his favorite superhero had ever seen, complete with all of its accessories.

Harry soon understood the operation of the well, and he began to play without wasting his time. The costume, like a bicycle, also disappeared after a time. Harry was happy. He waited patiently for the second gift from his well. It was his favorite comic. Harry and the dwarf had fun with all the wonderful gifts the well offered.

They were still in play when Harry was called. When they noticed Harry's absence, the Dwarfs began searching the woods for Harry. They came closer and the Dwarf ran after them. To show his gratitude, he gave Harry a beautifully wrapped gift and disappeared into a wooded area.

Soon Harry was found. He was careful not to let others know and kept the secret for himself. He did not open the gift, but waited patiently to find the best moment.

A few days later, when he opened it up, he discovered that it was a watch featuring a picture Harry playing near the water well. Harry felt disappointed and said to himself, "It's just a timepiece." I was sure it was too good a deal to be true that I would have a miniature version of that well.

He donned the watch anyway and began to watch TV. Within five minutes, the image of Harry playing happy was overthrown and a brand new picture emerged. This picture was Harry's bored, lonely self. Harry sat up straightening, and began to examine the watch carefully. Soon, he saw that the watch was changing every time he did nothing. He thought about what if minutes were gifts to be enjoyed just as gifts of well?

After realizing this, he began to use every moment of each day. It was like there had been multiple Harrys living in the house. He began studying, playing, learning new hobbies and even watching TV. It was not to pass the time, but with joy. He had already discovered the great gift of Time with its unending joy.

This was the end of Harry's story.

What number of adults can relate? I believe that almost everyone, at one time or another in their lives, understands the importance to manage time. Then, comes the struggle for new methods to manage time. Harry would be proud of their ending.

My son does not know that no Dwarves will guide us to this magical well of unending joy. We must also take all the necessary tools and equipment in order to find that special place. Some have already found it, while others still struggle to find it.

How to take advantage of all that life has to offer. How to live an enjoyable and healthy lifestyle with a better career, and happy relationships. How to take advantage of the best times? How to make most of your best days. Let's hope so!

Although the solution could be philosophical, we prefer to stick to our worldly methods.

Our primal ancestor didn't need to be reminded of hunting or gathering. Or eating and sleeping. Their lives were full of tasks that you could not ignore. But we've come so far in the years since then. From self-care to screaming deadlines, balancing relationships with countless meetings at the Workfront and not to mention the ever-attention-seeking social apps.

With so many things to do, our brain struggles with all the information. This is why we need to simplify. It categorizes all new information and then it starts to organize it. This worked great until there was a lot of urgent tasks. Because we now have limited time to work, our brain has to make choices about what next.

This has allowed for many different task management techniques, tips, tricks and technological advancements. Even now, with so many technological advancements at our fingertips, people still feel that they are behind others. They struggle to manage their time and find the right balance between work and personal life. But is this really true?

First, it's so easy to compare ourselves to others with the global network. It's not just us and our relations anymore which, in some ways, is absurd. It isn't like everyone is having a perfect life. We have seen it firsthand. They didn't wake-up like that.

So we arrive at our situation. Even though it is not comparable, there are still many things we need to do in a day.

This is when we begin to look at systems that make the most out of our time. How to make your life easier and more productive without stress?

Gary Keller, author of "The One Thing", explains that he often asks people their time management preferences when teaching productivity. He gets a lot of answers. Then, he continues to ask for the criteria that will determine the preferred system. The features are described by the people who describe the formats. He goes on to explain that how much money you make will determine how we use our time. Therefore, if time is money, the only way to describe a system is the money we make from using it. You can find how much money you make to identify the system you use. He states that the most productive people tend to be the most successful. However, he believes that the task management system does not end at creating lists and crossing them out.

This isn't about only chasing cash, it's about family life and good overall health.

It is the most irrevocable and precious gift that we have, making it the most precious. Time lost is time not lived as a fully human being, without experiencing, creative endeavor, enjoyment and suffering. ~ Dietrich Bonhoeffer

This approach to time will allow you to see how you can change your life. How do you go about doing that?

Glad that you asked!

You must shift your thinking. You and only you own your time. And you can choose what you do with your time. Stop telling yourself that you don't possess enough time. If you keep repeating the same phrase, you will begin to believe that it is impossible for you to control things.

It's possible to say you planned the perfect day but that your boss had some urgent work to do. You may feel that you have no other choice. It might seem like you don't have a choice. However, if you really think about it, you'll realize that the job you chose was yours and that with every decision you make you must also make some commitments.

If you have children and find it difficult to find time for yourself, there is no reason to. You chose to be a parent. You have chosen to dedicate your time to raising the next generation.

Lao Tzu, an antiquarian Chinese writer and philosopher, correctly explained the meaning behind this overused phrase. He said that Time is a creation. To say, "I don't need time" is to mean, "I don't want".

Laura Vanderkam gives a TED talk explaining that we all have enough time. Vanderkam states, "If your full-time job is 40 hours per week, you sleep eight hours a nights, which leaves 56 hours per week -- that leaves 72 free hours for other activities." Even if your main job is 50 hours a week or you have a side business, there are still 62 hours. Do you think 60 hours is enough? "That leaves 52 hours to do other things."

It's time that we have.

It's about priorities.

You need to establish priorities for your ambitions and your life priorities, and then start to work on them in order to make your life what you want.

But this is too vague. It's fine to dream big and have visions. They will not be realized if they aren't planned and executed.

And how do I do that?

We start planning our day.

It is important to make a list every day of the things you should be doing so that each day becomes part of your grand construction.

This is your life.

Execute them without fail. Many of the tasks on your list don't get done. It is scary and it is even worse for our brains.

Every failure will make you feel discouraged and the momentum for a productive future will slow down.

To create the perfect to-do lists, you must understand why so many people fail to make them, the neuroscience behind them, and why these popular methods work. Here are some psychological tips to help you be more productive and steps to create the perfect to-do list formula.

What we desire is a great, simple system that gives awesome results and balances our lives.

It's quite possible.

We recognize that others are doing the same. The successful are those who do not fail to try their best.

Now it is your turn.

You will discover your magic formula, which is unique to your life.

Chapter 2: Neuroscience Behind To-Do Lists

"We find out more about the workings of human brains. We are able to develop ideas to improve human brain function. Kevin Maney

It is easy to make a list, even though it seems inefficient to others. While this system has a long tradition, many today believe it is not as efficient. This idea is completely contrary to my opinion. No matter which system we follow making a list is the first step. These things are impossible to avoid. The truth is that we don't want them. Science has now caught up in the neuroscience of the brain, and is supporting our intuitive intuitions. It would be easier to accept the simple list if you understood the neuro-science aspects. Knowledge of neuroscience and the psychological aspects that underlie the lists can give you the knowledge to take control of your own time.

1. The brain categorizes all information that is presented to it:

Our brain is a remarkable machine. It is always trying to make sense out of the surrounding environment. When new information becomes available, it gets to work. After assessing the object's physical perception, it provides context and determines if it is worth more attention. It all happens seamlessly. When our brain already has decided the path to take, we don't even notice we are making a choice.

Walter Kintsch, Neuroscientist and Neuroscientist in 1968 pointed out that we tend to categorize. Walter Kintsch was an American professor emeritus of psychology at Colorado University. His revolutionary theories in cognitive psychology and text comprehension are well-known. He found that categorizing breaks down information into shorter and more distinct components.

When our brain perceives lists, it calls them organized information. It is spatially that processing happens. If we were to go grocery shopping, for instance, it would be difficult to remember the items. However, once you have a list of them, it's easier than ever to recall. Making notes for exams is another example. Writing in bullet points is more effective at recalling information than writing in paragraphs. It aids in immediate understanding and later recalls. You feel more intuitive.

2. Making lists will free you from the "Paradox of Choice"

Lists are also useful in removing the "paradoxof choices". Barry Schwartz published 'The Paradox of Choice: Why More Is Not Less' in 2004. Schwartz points out that shoppers can feel less anxious if they are able to eliminate their choices. The book examines the behaviour of different types people when they are confronted with the rich choice. The book then shows how the dramatic increase of choice--from the routines to the overwhelming difficulties of balancing personal and family needs- has paradoxically become both a problem and a solution. The paradox of choice is that we are more likely to choose what makes us feel worse. This is known as a paradox.

In 2011, Michaela Wanke and Claude Messner investigated how to relieve this feeling where there were more options than people can choose from. The investigation found that conscious work to process something makes us feel happier. There is a higher chance of us committing to something when we are aware of how long it will take.

Spend 5 minutes each night to plan the next day's activities and include it in your calendar. Then you won't have to get up every morning wondering what you should do. There is a clear outline of what the day will look like. It's not necessary to choose whether or not you should exercise, or what task you should complete first. It's easy to set up your schedule and task list, then go about completing it. You will feel happier if there are fewer options. To reduce the number of choices even further, choose what clothes to wear the next morning. Mark Zuckerberg and Steve Job, highly productive people, remove the choice of choosing by wearing a uniform. You will feel more productive if you have fewer options.

3. You would do it if you felt good about it.

The security that comes with a well-structured list of to-dos in your daily planner is both attractive and reassuring. Furthermore, the joy and satisfaction that comes from getting a job done strengthens the process and influences our future decisions. Robert Zajonc (social psychologist and well-known social psychologist) stated that preferences don't require inferences in his 1980 paper, "Feelings of Thinking". The main idea behind this paper was to show that not all feelings, or preferences, are based solely on cognitive processes. However, they can often be preceded by them. Impact doesn't necessarily require extensive cognitive processing. Simply put, you are more likely do something if there is a positive feeling about it. Then, we make choices based upon those preferences. We then give reasons why we made the right decisions.

I have a hard time thinking about the gym when I wake up every morning. Although they might be valid reasons, difficult to dismiss as excuses, the fact is I decided not to go to gym because it wasn't something I felt good about.

It sounds relatable, doesn't it?

There are certain things I enjoy doing, and they make me feel great, so I do them anyway. It's like reading, having coffee, or watching sci-fi movie. I don't need fact-based data to convince myself to do these things. I just need to get the important work done, and coffee boosts my productivity. The movie was my reward for getting things accomplished. It's hard to argue with the benefits of reading books. As Robert said, 'Preferences need no inferences.'

4. Planning clears your mind:

Recent studies confirm that the brain's short-term working memory is used for short-term storage of information. Bluma Zeigarnik, Russian psychologist, was the first to investigate this phenomenon. Her Professor Kurt Lewin, Gestalt psychologist and psychologist, had observed that waiters were better at retaining information about unpaid orders. But, once the task was finished and everyone had received their orders, it became clear that they were all paid. The waiter couldn't remember any additional details of the orders. Zeigarnik designed a series experiments to reveal the mechanism behind this phenomenon. She got participants to take part in many activities. They were only allowed to complete a few of the activities, and were then interrupted.

Participants were asked to list the activities that they have participated in after the activity had ended. Participants remembered activities that were interrupted twice as well as those they did get done. The brain still holds on to incomplete tasks, making it impossible for them to concentrate on other activities. This is known as Zeigarnik's effect. Her research was published in 1927 by Psychologische Forschung.

By simply writing down all the tasks, we can convince our subconscious mind that the task at hand is achievable. It frees our brainpower so that we can focus on other tasks.

Your subconscious brain stops nagging and considers activities that are planned as being addressed. It was discovered that those who had a plan as to how to tackle the issue, the steps involved, how they would carry it out, did not seem to be bothered about its incompletion.

Click Here to Get Your Free Planner Bundle

5. The brain functions best when it isn't required to remember the tasks.

McGill University Professor Daniel Levitin is a behavioral neuroscientist and psychologist. He wrote 'The Organized mind'. Our brain performs at its best when it is functioning optimally. Your brain's ability to store more will directly affect its performance. A list will allow you to concentrate on the task at hand. Danielle also stated that David Allen's GTD's biggest idea is the mind-clearing exercise of writing down all the talkter. However, he modified it to say that you don't need file everything as he suggested. According to him, some people like to file, while others prefer piles. Even the pilers can often find everything. He also stated that it is much easier to keep an assortment of files in a junk file than to spend precious time looking for these items.

Chapter 3: Why Did Your To Do List Fail?

"Complaining does not make things better in your life. Only actions will. Write down everything that needs to be done to improve the things you have going. Slowly, make those changes. Susan Jeffers

The trusty to-do list may seem simple, but many fail to implement it. There is a reason why 41% are left unfinished. It is no wonder that people develop a relationship with their lists. Susan said that complaining will not change the situation. Stop complaining about broken systems and find ways to make them work.

How can I master my to-do list?

They fail because they don't understand!

Before dismissing it as an ineffective tool that can be used for personal productivity, one must first understand the reasons behind it.

Address, master and understand.

If you don't take care of many things, a to-do listing can become a recipe for disaster. The following issues should be addressed.

1. Too lengthy to-do lists.

It is common to create a to-do checklist that is too long with all the things that must be completed. Problem is that we only have 24 hours per day. You must eat, sleep, exercise, as well as do other important things. Family and friends are the ones to whom we have given our time. You cannot work 24 hours a day with all these people. Only a small number of tasks can be accomplished in that amount time. Simply dumping everything in your head into a list won't make you more productive. This is simply a brain-dumplist. Not a to-do list.

A long list is something that's very common. You won't be able complete it in the time you set. It can lead to a negative feedback loop.

2. No prior prioritizing.

The master list is a good starting point, but it should not be the only one. It is easier to do jobs that are not important if you don't prioritize and add context. These tasks will require less effort.

You might decide that writing back to an e-mail is on your list, but not in alignment with the long-term goal. You get addicted to the dopamine rush, which gives off an immediate high. You can become frustrated when you see the growing list of things to do and are unable to reach your life goals. Although you may feel productive, you don't feel productive. It is also known as the productivity paradox.

3. Manpower and energy are not enough

Your perfect method of managing your task may be a formula that you have created. You might also have a list to protest with realistic deadlines. However, you feel exhausted. To reach your goals, you will need to have the energy to carry out your tasks and the willpower to keep going even when it's not easy. There will be moments when you feel like giving up.

Know your body, and learn to listen to it. To help your body achieve what you want, you need to befriend it. Some people have the best energy and willpower available in the morning. Some perform better at night. Utilize that energy to finish the important task first. You should not waste energy on tasks you don't need, even though they might seem urgent.

4. No deadlines.

A long list of tasks, without any deadlines, invites procrastination. Effective formulas have deadlines. We all know where our energies should be focused. You may have some tasks on your mind that you need to complete. But you don't. why?

Because you realize there's still plenty of time. Remember when college assignments were due, the majority used to finish them. Just before the deadlines or right on them.

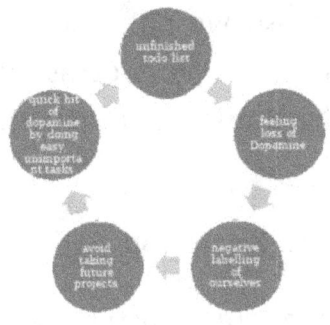

Parkinson's Law is at the root of all this. This law states that work increases in proportion to the time taken to do it.

However, knowing this doesn't make it easy to do. You must aim to be conscious at the stage when all tasks are completed within the specified time. The best and worst things about adulthood are that we have the freedom to do whatever we please. This means you don't need to ask permission to enjoy an extra scoop in your favorite icecream flavor. It means you only have the power to make your body work harder and stop snacking.

This is the reason our lists end up failing. Our lists fail because we don't set deadlines for projects and tasks. We procrastinate, fail and get caught in the horrible negative feedback loop.

5. Negative feedback loop

Not only is it a stress-buster, but so is the joy of completing a list. This won't make us more productive, even though we might like it. But, it has a positive effect on us over the medium and long term.

Feeling worse about yourself is caused by the unmanageable number of tasks we can accomplish each day on our To-Do List. The negative feedback loop that results from our To-Do list growing longer than shorter is a vicious one.

What's the current situation?

Feeling dopamine deprivation from unfinished tasks can cause us to feel numb. This is why we tend to be more focused on the unfinished list than what has been accomplished. This makes us feel over-analytical and leads us to conclude that we have something wrong. We begin to label ourselves lazy, disorganized, or all over. It happens when subconsciously, we stop taking on new projects to improve our self-esteem. We are prone to taking a quick dose of dopamine, clearing out our email and checking social media. And so the loop continues.

Our brain is predisposed to focusing more on negative circumstances than positive ones.

This trait saved a lot of lives during evolution, when there was more danger. Our ancestors managed to remain safe by focusing on the right situations and avoiding them.

Chapter 4: Composition Of Perfect Productivity

The road to the place where magic happens requires some milestones. To create the perfect To-Do List, you need to go through them.

Even before that, I believe that one perfect system is a myth. There is no one single system that is perfect for everyone. There is no universal truth regardless of your job, schedule, culture, etc. The vast amount of information available about task management systems is overwhelming. Some principles have been proven to be effective over time. However, we need a better system that meets our specific needs. Your approach will be more focused, productive, stress-free, and precise the more you refine it.

Now you are able to see how to succeed. However, this is only the beginning. We also want all that this simple tool can offer.

There are key ingredients in the formula. This chapter will be about how to incorporate them into the formula. These steps are important. Take the time to review them. These are the important ingredients.

1. Realistic goals

People underestimate what they can achieve in a single day. They tend to overestimate their abilities and pile on too many tasks.

They don't complete the list in one day so it keeps growing.

2. Poor prioritization.

Few people receive formal training for task management. Many people see a to do list as a dump of all the things they have in their heads. This approach won't get you very far. Even if you're an advanced user, there's a chance that you pick simpler tasks that can be completed in minutes. As we've seen in the "Idonethis" reports. This will lead to a false sense in productivity, and you'll be one day less from achieving your long term goal.

The key is prioritizing to get the right results.

It is impossible to have a productive and stress-free life if you don't finish your to-dos in order of importance.

3. Time-bound execution.

Procrastination is a common sin.

Most people are guilty of procrastinating. Setting deadlines for your task is the best thing to do.

Even if your project does not have a deadline, you can give it one.

Tim Urban, the creator of "wait, however why", presented a Tedtalk entitled "Inside a master procrastinator'. Tim Urban wanted a deeper understanding of why procrastination is so bad for us.

His talk was both amusing and eye-opening. He explained that there are two types: people who procrastinate and people who don't. Both have a rational brain that makes decisions, but the brains of both procrastinators and those who do not are able to handle this instant gratification monkey. It can make it hard to focus on important work while making it fun and easy. This gratification monkey causes the procrastinator to ignore the rational side of his brain.

The panic monster, which is awakened at the sight of a deadline, is what keeps this monkey going. While this puts the rational decision-maker back in control, it creates unnecessary pressure. Tim stressed that procrastination cannot be avoided by setting deadlines. To emphasize this point, Tim pulled out a 100 year calendar and asked "What exactly are you procrastinating?"

He concluded that you should act now if it's something that is helping you reach your goals.

4. Automation and delegation

Automation and technology can be used to automate more tasks in a stress-free manner. You can find a solution for your problem by looking online. Then, invest in the tools you need to save your time.

To make it easier to do more, share your workload. You can't do everything with machines. Some tasks require human insight and intellect. One must be honest with oneself here. To delegate, one must not be in complete control. It might not happen the way you had hoped, but it will.

5. Actionable Tasks

To-do-lists will only work as well as you make them. A task you've given is unclear and lacking context. You will not be able complete it.

It is important to put tasks in an actionable phrase when using t0-dos. You can break down your task, for example, to plan a party for your son. Then, put them in your calendar. If you don't do this, your mind won't stop looking at your list. It will cause you to become distracted by other things and push you towards urgent tasks that may seem more pressing.

6. Be aware of when to stop and continue on the next day.

Our goal is to make life easy by creating a list of everything we need. It's good to keep a list and to stick to it, but this can lead to more stress in order to accomplish everything. This is a bad practice that can lead to productivity and loss of peace of mind. Everyone should be able accomplish their tasks. If there are any remaining tasks, you can adjust them to your next day's or weekly schedule. Don't get mad at yourself. It happens. Give yourself a break.

Chapter 5: Top 10 Task Management Systems

"They say time changes everything. But you must actually change them yourself." Andy Warhol

The human quest for more and greater is not new. Not just the discovery of fire, however, was the end. Humans continued to improve on their primitive methods and today we have the most innovative appliances in our kitchen section. Also, verbal and written messages have been replaced by telephones and telegraphs. We've made a lot of progress. You know we're not going to stop there. Because we are wired. We can find solutions, then improvise on them. This may be why we are able to dominate the planet despite lacking brute strength, or mammoth structural structure.

These changes and our quest for perfection in every aspect of our lives are exhausting and stressful. Even if we just want to live a normal life, it's more hectic than ever. So many things to do and so little time. What did we do? We learned how to manage our time. We understood that everyone has 24 hours per day. It was how we manage them that is the key to success.

Many people attempted it on their own, but we stayed with some of the task management methods. This could be due to the simplicity, clarity, or efficiency of these methods.

It is good to seek out the perfect formula. However, it would make more sense if we could learn from the wise men who spoke about time management. Instead of reinventing everything, we can just go down the aisle to look at them all, grab the right ingredients, then create the perfect recipe for managing our lives stress-free.

Many of these you will be familiar with. You may have even tried them all. You might have heard of certain methods, but you aren't sure if they work for you. It is not our intention to deny the principles, but to be able to compare the pros and con of each system and determine which one works best.

It would be great to learn what is wrong with the approach, and why people don't complete their to do lists. There are many options when it comes to task management systems. For simplicity and clarity we will stick with the most popular and determine their effectiveness.

This is the complete list:

1. The all-inclusive masterlist technique

2. Method for completing tasks within deadlines

3. The master list, daily to-do and daily to list method

4. The 3+2 System

5. The 1-3-5 Strategy

6. Project-Based System

7. The 3 MIT Method

8. Kanban methodology

9. The Eisenhower Box

10. David Allen - Getting things done

The all-inclusive masterlist technique

This name says it all. It's a huge list with every task, every reminder and every idea.

This is done to help the brain get rid of all the annoying thoughts in the subconscious. The method isn't a system, and can be used by anyone who isn't familiar with the task management system. As each day brings in new tasks and things, the problem with this list is that it will be impossible to complete. You will lose your motivation to finish the list, and it is likely that you won't start any tasks from the list.

All of this reference will result in decision fatigue. It can leave you feeling indecisive as to what your next move should be. This is a surefire recipe for disaster. People will tend to do the easiest and then give up. People will abandon urgent and vital tasks and simply cross the item off the list. Do you not agree that this is the right thing for successful people to do? This is exactly what we should abstain from.

The lack of priority assignments is also detrimental to long-term achievement.

It is not without merits as it is the first step to creating that perfect formula. First, write down all of the details. Next organize the list by priority, context and other elements.

The task with deadlines method

It is an improvement on the all-inclusive large master list method. Users can then write down tasks and prioritize them, putting the start/due date at the beginning of each task. This task management system is easy to follow and can be used to save time, as it gives enough time for both starting and finishing the task.

If you are aware of the deadlines for a particular project or task, it is easier to keep it on track and take prompt action. With the ability to assign a starting date, you can put your focus on the tasks that matter most and not waste time working on other lists. This small modification to an all-inclusive masterlist will increase productivity. Your precious resources can be used to complete tasks that are currently being completed or that must be started that day. Say 'NO!' to wasting your energy on future tasks.

The master list, daily to-do and daily to list methods

The name of this method implies that it consists two lists. One master list that contains everything you need, all the projects due, your goals for the future, etc.

No matter whether you are writing a book or learning a guitar, your master list will include a trip to the supermarket and a long-due call to your parents. Now you have your master checklist. The master list is what you will use to review your work periodically. Make sure to review it at least once daily. You will select tasks from your ever-growing master list that are urgent and must be completed in the near future according your limited time.

Your master list won't be complete. It is there to save your from lots of tedious memorizing. You should never try to finish it all. Your daily tasks may be small and you don't want to have to finish them all.

It's as simple as that.

You can choose to use your preferred method. It could be a pen or paper, or a digital application. Put down everything you want. Don't be concerned about the order or length of your list. It might seem ridiculous to you because of how random it turns out, but that's perfectly normal. The problem is solved and your brain is free to think about it. Then, move on the second list.

This is your daily to-do list.

Now, go through the master checklist and choose the important tasks. They should be added to your list according to priority and when they must be completed.

This is a good way not to get overwhelmed by a huge Master list and help you finish your tasks more realistically.

You might even consider planning for several days instead of just a daily overview.

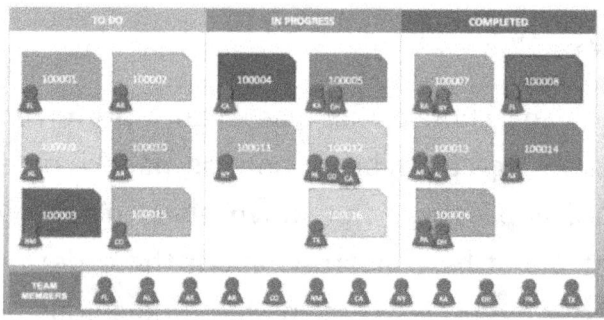

The 3+2 System

This system works better than any of the others because it focuses on just five tasks daily. Three big tasks and two smaller ones. You may now wonder how a task is categorized as being large or small. It is based on the amount time required to complete it. A major task can be completed in an hour. For smaller tasks, you can finish them in 30 minutes. You can break down a more difficult task into smaller tasks, and then tackle each one one at a later time.

This system's strength lies in the fact that it only has a few tasks. If you can clearly see what you have to accomplish each day, it will make it less tempting to switch tasks. It may not seem like much but switching tasks can make it difficult to focus and increase efficiency. Because of the scope of this to-do, there's no risk of decision fatigue. Even better, pseudo-productivity can be avoided in areas where you may feel productive, such answering emails or updating your social media accounts. However, this won't help you achieve your long-term and short term goals.

The system also has its flaws. This system does not mention the master lists or the times to review the daily tasks. Do you need to think about your daily to-do list? You will find a certain amount of rigidity in this system, as the number of tasks you can address is only five. This system is a good first step towards completing more tasks, but it's incomplete.

The 1-3-5 Strategy

To make the '3+2' system more efficient and flexible, the 1-3-5 strategy can be extrapolated from the previous method of task-management. This strategy will let you

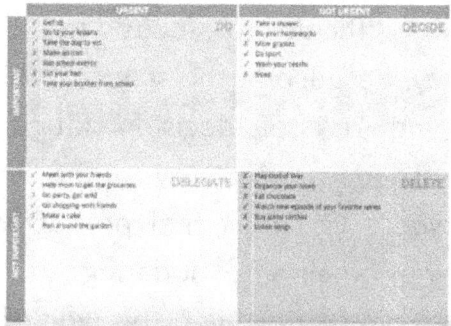

schedule one large, three medium-sized and five small tasks.

Instead of only five tasks in the 3-2 System, you can accomplish nine tasks here.

The strategy seeks to reduce rigidity while adding medium-sized jobs. This is good news, as many tasks may not qualify as a major task. Not small enough to take 30 minutes. You'll be able manage your schedule better this way.

Consider what to do if you need to tackle a task that will take 45 minutes. If you are following the 3+2 Method, this task cannot be included in your daily schedule. It is possible to have a greater chance at finishing it if you use a 1-3-5 strategy.

The downsides and benefits of the 3+2 method can also be seen here. It's an improved version, and can be modified to make this even more efficient.

Project-Based System

Many unsuccessful task management systems fail because they don't include context in the to-do lists. This issue is addressed with the project-based method. This system doesn't allow you to choose random tasks you need to complete daily. Instead, it allows you to select the projects that interest you and then create a list. You can break down each segment into manageable segments.

To plan your vacation, make a list with items such as the following.

1. Plan the budget.

2. The length of your vacation

3. Determine the destination based on your time and financial resources.

4. Do your research on the markets and sights.

5. Book the hotel

6. Buy your air/train tickets.

7. You can plan the daily itinerary.

8. Pack according the weather of your destination.

9. List all the things that you may need.

10. Make sure you have everything covered while you're on vacation.

The list will contain all your projects. Each time you wish to accomplish a task, you will refer back to that list and move on to the next.

This system offers a great view from the sky of each project. This is especially useful for those who want to track the progress on multiple projects at once.

You may have guessed it by now.

This is far from the best way to increase productivity without stress.

It's up to us how we structure our days. Each day will be different and you have to choose which ones. You should not limit your productivity by following a single task list. This is bad for your brainpower. Your brainpower will be depleted if you switch between decision-making and switching.

Without the need for day-structuring this project-based method may help you get on the right track. However, it will also provide a context-based framework that can be used to improve other areas of your daily life. As well as peace and health.

The 3 MIT Method

Although it is not clear where the original method came from, Leo Babauta (zenhabits.net) has helped to popularize the idea for improving productivity and enhancing daily life.

This is probably the one you came across as you were trying to optimize your workday. MIT stands to represent 'most important task'. This approach is designed to help you focus more effectively. Focusing only on one task will help you have more neuro-resources. This will also reduce switching costs. It's much easier to integrate it into your busy schedule. It's easier than ever to accomplish your to-do items, which is also a dopamine booster to keep you on the right track.

This was originally about finishing a single thing per day. 'Most important thing'. One thing is the most important, can't it?

A little twist on the original method is 3 MIT, which suits better today's fast-paced environment. As we all have so many tasks, this is more practical. Pick three priorities and then commit to finishing them all in one day.

One might wonder, after learning about the 3+2 method or the 1+3+5 approach, how can one decide the time to allocate to each task? The MITs can be completed in less time, leaving you plenty of time. These MITs might require you to do a lot of work and be exhausting.

This allows the user complete control over the process. It's open-ended in this way. Once you have the system's framework and approach, the details are up to you. It's possible to adjust the system to fit your project and timetable. This can lead to people becoming frustrated with their task management system and losing trust in it. Too much freedom can cause you to lose your focus and allow you to relax.

How do you decide which tasks are most important? Or when to go over it? How to add this system to your calendar so you can get more done. There are many more possibilities when you start following this method.

Nonetheless, this is a fantastic approach to consider when you are creating your ultimate formula for the to do list.

Kanban methodology

Kanban follows a visual system. This allows you to keep track of your to-dos, assess your progress on undergoing tasks, as well as see how they are getting done.

Here are the steps to get you started.

A corkboard should have three columns. You can use a stack to keep track of all your tasks. You can do only one task per post-it. The columns should now be titled from left to right. The first column will be called "To-Do", followed by the middle as "In Progress", and then the last as "Completed". Put all of your task-written posts-its in the "To-Do" column. As you probably guessed now. You will then need to shift them according the their respective stages.

Kanban Board

It is a fantastic way to prioritize tasks. You are instantly informed about urgent and critical tasks. It shows you a visual representation that confirms the status of any task. You can see the tasks that you need to tackle, which projects are currently in process and what you have achieved so far.

Another advantage is that you can organize your tasks according your priority. You might try combining a few features from different approaches to make your method unique.

An alternative is to use a dry erase board, or you can even use multiple apps online if you prefer. Apps such KanbanFlow or Leankit, Kanbanote, and Trello are some examples.

The Kanban method is not without its weaknesses. It can hinder the Kanban process if there is a master checklist with multiple tasks. Multitasking can be complicated and you must keep tabs on multiple items at once. High-value tasks can be overlooked if you just ignore the "To Do" column.

The Eisenhower Box

Stephen Covey is the author of "The Seven Habits of Highly Effective People," a highly acclaimed book. He popularized the method, which follows the principles of the matrix system. This tool can be used to allocate time for competing tasks.

It is important to first create a matrix with 4 quadrants.

1. Important + Urgent

2. Important + Not Urgent

3. Not Important + Urgent

4. Not Important + Not Urgent

The next step is to organize the tasks according to priority. Prioritize the tasks that are 'Important+ Urgent' in the first quadrant. They need to be addressed immediately. The second quadrant includes important, but not urgent things that can be done immediately or in the future. Tasks in the third quadrant are referred to as 'Not important + urgent'. The last quadrant is for tasks that are not urgent or important and can be delegated.

This matrix system allows you to quickly identify your most urgent tasks, as well as those tasks that can be abandoned easily. It encourages aligning your tasks with long-term goals. This will ensure that you only spend time on high-value tasks and that you don't feel guilty about removing tasks from your larger picture.

It is possible to mistakenly believe that this is the best method to manage your tasks. This method is amazing, but you might be disappointed by the lack or context, time needed to accomplish tasks, the connections between tasks and too many options. These factors can lead to a ruined day.

David Allen - Getting things done

David Allen is a productivity expert with a huge following. He was the author of 'Getting Things Done,' which is widely known as the best book on task management. This method teaches that your mind is not meant to hold ideas but rather for having them. The idea is that your mind is for having new ideas and not for holding them. All the other stuff floating around your head just gets lost in the shuffle. It is stressful to be unable to categorize in terms context, priority, intended outcomes.

GTD requires that you first put these random thoughts into a list. Then, each item can be actionable. You can organize each item according its context from this master list. This means you will need to create multiple lists. You will then need to place them where you want them. To stay on top of the system, you should review it every week.

This is GTD for you. It's a comprehensive system. Many books have been written on the subject, which proves its usefulness in chaotic times like today.

This article will help you to identify the features of a well-designed task management system.

First, by creating a new list from your master list, each item will have context.

They are then being separated again according to their importance. The tasks needed to be placed on the "next actions", and "someday/maybe" list. This system lets you focus on important tasks while allowing you to save time and allow you to collect ideas that could have value in the near future. The "someday/maybe" list contains ideas that can be further evaluated.

The third aspect is the focus on weekly review. David Allen refers it as an important step to the successful inclusion GTD. The fourth essential feature is to give you enough freedom and structure to make your system.

This is the most famous strategy for getting things done. However, it is not perfect and many of its early followers became disillusioned.

Even though it has all the characteristics of a great method, the GTD approach is not enough in many ways. Although it can be very helpful, it doesn't make you stress-free until you are able to get all your clutter out of your head and onto paper. Once that happens, you can be certain of its effectiveness. But as they start to lose faith in the method, they begin to see the shortcomings.

The system is lacking a strong focus on 'purpose. Focusing on the long term goal keeps you motivated and focused. You can measure your progress by achieving your goals. GTD emphasizes productivity but fails to include fulfillment.

That's it!

With the knowledge of most task management systems available, you can now move forward and create your perfect to-do listing. Next is to find out what the key features are to remember when creating your to-do list. This will determine whether or not it will be completed.

Chapter 6: How To Balance Work And Life
Michelle Obama

You work, then you come home to get ready for work the next day. Work schedules can impact your family's commitments and household chores.

It's possible to be successful at anything you choose, but there is no guarantee that you'll find happiness. A human being isn't a robot. You know deep within that you are very far away from what you love. You might think it's your relationships. It could also be your long-term dreams or your mental peace.

Is there a time block in your daily life that you don't have the energy to do what you were passionate about growing up? Are you able to make time for your loved ones? Do you feel that you are living life to its fullest potential? ?

If the answer is 'No,' then you should balance your home and work life. Simple, but not easy for all.

The key to achieving that balance is to manage your time.

But how do we do that?

The common understanding is that time management does not include life management. If one does not know how to manage his or her life, it is impossible to manage it. Your choice in life management. Understanding the distinction is not easy. It doesn't mean that you are successful. You might be able earn money well but your family and personal lives will not be satisfactory. What would you consider success?

Common excuses are that it is hard to manage time. This is a mistaken approach. If you really desire to live a happy life, and you have the right attitude you'll be able do your best in all aspects of it. The first step towards a better lifestyle is to set priorities. It means you will do what you should, and no time wasters.

How to decide priorities

We all know that you need 7 hours of sleep. How many of us exercise and eat well at the correct times? How many of you are open to six simple joys that allow you to do more than just work?

Similar to how you create a daily list that outlines your priorities at work, you can also make another list listing the most important things that you want do with your family. Mary Kay Ash.

Many times I have skipped lunch. I was also working well past midnight to finish my projects in time for the deadline. I procrastinated and only wanted my time to do the work until the eleventh hour. I used say to myself, "I work best when I'm under pressure." It was just a way of justifying my actions. I know deep down that this is a lie.

After my son was born, everything changed. I had the task of deciding my priorities. I am unable to work late at night, in order to sleep in. I do not get that two hour extra sleep. My baby's schedule was the basis of my home. His routine was all I had to do in my daily planner. He needed to be fed, pooped, washed, and had his play time. As a mother, he is my main priority. But I had to keep my other commitments in order. This was the best thing I could do for myself at the moment.

Yasmin Da'Souza & Amitabh Sinha had a book about it that I was interested in. I found a formula there that I liked. I modified it according to my own needs. After a few weeks, my life was back on the right track. It's yours to play with, so take it!

You can always change it. Keep in mind that nothing is fixed and you can change it at any time.

It is important to first categorize key areas of your life. Get a piece if paper and note down the ones that will reward you most.

1. Carrier

2. Family

3. Financial

4. Education

5. Physical fitness

6. Social life

7. Relationships

8. Recreation

9. Personal time

You can also list out your priorities. Then, give them to school. One is the lowest and ten the highest. Now, sort them by the results.

Here's how it would look if I made a checklist.

SCORE OF PRIORITY

Family 10

Reading 8

4. Eat Four

Sleeping 9

Exercise 5

Communication 1

6

Meditation 7

PRIORITY SCORE

Writing 3

Travelling 2

Place the items according to their score. Now you can see which areas are my most important. I will limit my time to the top three to five priority areas. The rest of the tasks can be delegated or deleted.

These are my priorities sorted in order of score.

SCORE OF PRIORITY

Family 10

Sleeping 9

8.

Meditation 7

6

These are my top 10 priorities and they bring me the most rewards. Only now, I must add them to my schedule so that I don't have to worry about any other tasks or projects.

My list may not be ideal, but it worked for me. My son will soon be a big brother and sister. Naturally, family is at the top of my list. The second is sleep. Motherhood, as joyful and wonderful as it is, comes with its challenges. The number one challenge is sleep deprivation. If I am not sleeping well, I won't feel at my best to enjoy my family and friends time. Additionally, my body had to recover from giving birth and repair itself.

Reading is the third. I love to read. In addition to all the health benefits you might reap from reading a good book, I find that it is almost meditative. There were days when I couldn't find the time, and it was difficult to see the light from this perspective. Reading was the only way to get more focused, organized, and calm. While music and running may sound like music to some, it's for me reading. This is why I now make it a point to read.

Meditation is the next item on this list. One might be curious as to why I stress meditation when I read that it is calm and joyful. The key is to be able to see the bigger picture by looking inward. The hard lesson I learned was that you can't be happy even if everything goes well. While I am aware that this book is intended to increase productivity and manage time, all that matters is if you feel like there's no point in doing it.

The motivational videos you watch and the speeches you hear will eventually wear off and your life will return to normal. True inspiration comes within. Meditation helps me see my future, past, and present. What do I want to live my life like? Then I start to work on achieving it. If I feel disoriented or missing something, all I have to do is ask: "What do you want?"

When I get that answer I use all productivity strategies to manage my time and make space for my future goals.

Last, but not least is work. There are nine to five jobs for people, as well as a business or other dedicated work hours. It makes it easier to make time in their schedule. People who are freelancers or like me, have to be more disciplined.

You need to decide how much time you are willing to dedicate to each priority. Let's look at my list.

Priority Average time Total hours

1. Family 2 hours A.M. - 4 hrs P.M.

2. Sleeping 7.30 - 8hrs 8 hours

3. Reading 1 Hour P.M. 1 Hour

4. Meditation 20-30 minutes 30 minutes

5. 2-hour workday

Every night, I get between 7:30 and 8 hours of sleep. I need time to rest before I fall asleep.

To do this, I add an additional half an hour to the schedule. One hour of solid family time and around half an hours of meditation. I also have four hours to work on the career. So, 19.5 hours is a total of 24 hours each day.

I will need to use the bathroom and eat so please allow one to two more hours. This would allow me to work for two more hours.

In the two hours, I could exercise, walk in nature and call my friends. I could also watch movies, go shopping or write a book. If I don't feel like doing something, I can just check my Instagram and Facebook accounts. It is brilliant!

You won't be doing this all seven days.

I also suggest just do a quick life assessment. The score will be based on your life in general, such as health, finances, love and mental well-being, and other areas. Look at where you can focus your efforts to be your best next day and next week.

Rinse again.

Chapter 7: Formulation Your Perfect To Do List

There is time for certain things, and time for all things. There is time for great things and time for small things. ~ Miguel de Cervantes

We now have all the knowledge we need to be able to use these systems to get to our formula. It's important to note that not everyone can have the same kind of schedule. Due to the constant changes in life, you might find different formulae at different times.

I used to study 12 hours a week to prepare for exams. Now, I sit down for 6 hours twice daily. From 10 to 4. Both AM/PM. I was able learn all subjects within six months. But, this was the moment when I didn't need to worry about buying groceries or cooking. My only job was studying. It was hard on my body. It worked, as you can see from my academic achievements. After that, my life was a complete change. I had to manage the household and take over for my parents. I knew that I would have to study six hours per day for six months to pass any national-level competitive exam. My schedule has changed completely. I divided my time so I could study for 2 hours in the morning and 2 in the afternoon. This worked well for me. Even though I now have a toddler boy, and many other things as every human being on the planet to take care of, I have made a complete shift in my daily schedule. I'm no longer a night owl but a morning-bird. This schedule fits my needs because it allows me to have three hours of solitude before the madness begins. This schedule has allowed me to complete my doctorate, finish a book, keep my reading habits and most importantly, my sanity.

While I can confidently say that this formula works, it is likely to change according your current circumstances. You must be aware of your personal life before you put things in order. If the process seems too complicated, you can always re-visit it. Perhaps you have achieved whatever you wanted in that stage of your life. I can now read for pleasure and not for hours of study. You might also have the opportunity to get that project done, have your dream job, or even married. Your ideal life will include a relocation, a new baby, or some order in your seemingly chaotic life. You will adapt your formula. Do not throw it out. Instead, modify it according to your requirements.

Let's begin mixing all ingredients together until we find the perfect combination.

1. Make a list.

First, write down everything. The first system we look at is not perfect but it is a good starting point. You can now put all of the thoughts and musings that go through your head on paper or online. The deadline is approaching, so book a table on date night, set up a tap, as well as all your long-term goals.

It is possible to reduce stress by suppressing your subconscious. You may be familiar with the Zeigarnik phenomenon. You might find it working for you.

Do not be afraid of making a big list. This master list is your responsibility and can easily get out of control. Some people may receive 150-200 tasks. Let it be that way, but don't let this intimidate you. This is your first step on the thousand-mile journey.

2. Pay attention to how you spend your time.

Prior to managing your time, it is important that you manage yourself. Productivity does not come at the expense of being disciplined with time-wasters. Knowing what you do to your time will help you know where your time is going. This will be done using the Eisenhower diagram. The one with all four quadrants.

Take a look at your day, and record everything you do in each quadrant. Sometimes what may seem urgent or necessary might not be as important in retrospect. Maybe you think you'll just check once on your social media but then you scroll through the entire thing for 45 minutes. You might have an excuse, but those 45 minutes will be covered in the last quadrant. Eliminating this task will give you 45 minutes to do what really matters.

You shouldn't stop checking these websites. These platforms must be regularly checked. Only after you've made a decision, and only for that time. That will give you greater control of the day.

It can take some time to figure out the 24 hour hours of your day. Your daily schedule changes from Monday to Thursday. Many people are surprised that Saturdays or Sundays can vary. It may take a few weeks.

And brutal honesty.

Follow the steps and you will become more informed. The powerful matrix will help you to identify where you spend your time. This will allow you to be more productive.

Knowledge is power. You know what you now have and it's your turn to feel that power.

3. Manage, delegate.

The next step in your journey is to get rid of all the time you spend on it. Analyze the quadrants. Find out how many can be eliminated with minimal adverse impact. (There goes quadrant 4!)

How many people can be delegated? You could ask someone else to step in or hire someone else to complete the task.

It is imperative to note that this task could be automated or deleted before you hire someone. If you do not, you're wasting your time as well as your hard-earned dollars.

You can only do the urgent tasks. Rory Vaden offers a simple way to manage our time. Rory is a Nashville-based executive consultant.

Ted Talk, "How do you multiply your time?" He mentions that other than making lists and prioritizing things, and assigning values based on urgency or importance, there is an additional element important which has a much greater impact on our time management.

He recommends that you ask the following questions to free up your time:

1. This task can be eliminated.

2. If it's not possible to remove it, can it still be automated?

3. Can it be delegated? Or can I show someone how to do it myself?

4. What should I do?

These questions will test your ability to plan. After applying this method you will have lots of time left over and can only do urgent or imporant tasks.

Here's a list of essential tasks. The next step in this process is to make a daily schedule.

4. Daily To-Do List

It's time for the rubber on the road. A daily to-do-list is a good idea. It will include all the necessary tasks and their deadlines. You can use any type of application or a physical list. The list must be able to hold you. It is not enough to fill it with all the things that you need. You want to make it a sustainable system, not a burnout diet. Applying this method will ensure that the time you have is used well.

To see the tasks at different times throughout the day, group them under the categories of homework/personal. It is a good idea that you keep all your tasks in one location. This can be a notebook, your smartphone, or any other app.

The effort that you put into a to-do list will only make it work. We know now that having an ideal to-do list won't help us get things done. If we don't have the willpower or energy to finish it, then we won't be able to make them happen. It's better for us to concentrate our energy on the most important task. This can change the negative feedback into a positive one. This is why we use the 80/20 Rule.

5. Pareto's principal, or 80/20 rule

To complete the most important tasks first, it is important to know what the most important tasks are.

This question is subjective. To help you get started, it is important to complete tasks that exponentially decrease your workload. Remember Pareto's rule of 80/20, also known as the 80/20 principle.

Joseph M. Juran is a management consultant who proposed the idea in the context of quality controls and improvement. Vilfredo Paraeto, an Italian economist was his inspiration. Pareto spotted the 80/20 connection in Lausanne while he was studying at the University of Lausanne. Vilfredo's first book, 'Cours d'economie politique', revealed that only 20% of Italy's land was owned.

Pareto Principle states that for most outcomes, approximately 80% of consequences are due to 20% of the causes. The "vital few" is around 20%. Imperatively 20 percent of your actions lead to 80% of the results. Therefore, it is important to finish tasks that produce the highest results.

This principle is also known to be the 80/20 law, the law governing the vital few, and the principle of factor sparsity. This is an extremely practical and useful rule that has stood the test. This is the basic idea. Here's the deal.

The first thing you need to do is take a close look at your list. Next, evaluate the weight of each task. You will see that not all tasks are equally important. However, some tasks have greater impact. Next, pick those that are most important and then list them according to the 80/20 rule. Also, urgent and critical tasks tend to be more time-sensitive. If you have to do a task that is dependent on another member of your team, prioritize it for them.

To get things done, you need to list them in an order that is manageable." Robert Breault

The goal of our work is to accomplish the most valuable task first. This is the only way to reach new heights. We've noticed that our to-do lists are often long and we tend to be more productive if we finish them faster. This is due to dopamine being released, but it can negatively impact productivity. To achieve the right balance between daily productivity, and long-term success, we need to prioritize tasks.

6. Pick the method that you prefer.

Our formula was universal until this point. We can now adapt the formula to your individual needs.

Don't worry about the time taken. Once the formula has been developed, it will stay with you for a lifetime. It's worthwhile.

Pick the number. The maximum number of tasks you can accomplish successfully.

It could be 1+3+5, 3+2, 3, or 3 MITs. You can even do one if you are very busy.

You don't have to pick a small number of people because you're lazy. You can stay motivated by being realistic with yourself, your energy, and your willpower. The best thing for you is to choose one thing. Seeing it reach its completion daily will give you the motivation to keep going. It is easy to set high goals but fail to reach them.

Martin Luther King Junior stated that "If you are unable to fly then run" and "If you cannot run then walk if your legs can't support you walking then crawl." However, no matter what you do, you need to keep moving forward.

You can make progress by moving closer to your goals. You must understand it, then you must implement it.

As you achieve more success, your time will be more manageable and you can choose to tackle more things.

7. Calendar

(The Most Important Subcomponent)

This is the critical step and the climax in our movie. It is essential for your success. We have our master and refined lists. The 80/20 rule has been applied to our list. And we have decided how many tasks we want each day.

So far, so good.

These steps won't be worth anything if we can't achieve the right.

How to do this?

They can be scheduled!

Chris Bailey is a productivity expert who gave a Ted Talk entitled "A more humane approach to productivity" in 2016. Chris gave the example of being busy, but not productive. While our calendar may be cluttered with a lot of things, how many entries actually help us move closer to our goals. Many of us have experienced this kind of quagmire. We waste our time doing things that are not really important. He suggested that you focus your attention and energy on the top three items for the day.

This step is crucial. If you are aware that you must complete five tasks per day, but you have other commitments, this is not a good idea. Even the best methods will go to the trashcan.

Look through your calendar to find out when your task is due and then place it there.

Our brain is more able to follow clear instructions. It is easier for our brain to follow clear instructions than procrastination.

If you use different devices, sync your calendars with the other device and keep them in line. Protect your time from any other wasteful activities if necessary.

Once you begin to see the benefits it has for productivity, you will continue to practice it. By following it faithfully, you will eventually develop the habit and routine of sticking to your calendar.

Click Here to Get Your Free Planner Bundle

8. Check the system each week.

All of these efforts will help you manage your life in a productive and stress-free way. But, to maintain this system, you must periodically review it. The recommendation is to review it once a week.

Every Sunday morning, get out your tablet or pen and write down all tasks. The daily goals should correspond with your weekly goals. The weekly goals should correspond to your monthly goal.

Don't get overwhelmed. Start small. Set a weekly goal and add it to the calendar. You will then be able to review your progress and make sure that you have done all the right things. next week similar drill.

It will get easier as you age.

Robin Sharma said it in his book "The leader who had no title" that "Change is the hardest at beginning, most difficult in middle and best at end." I keep reminding myself of this quote.

Chapter 8: Top 6 Productivity Enhancer Tips
Jean de La Fontaine

In the middle of the 1920s, a Michigan executive was looking at the efficiency and productivity his factory workers. He noticed that their proficiency was dropping when they worked too many working hours or too many work days. He instituted new policies and regulations. He stated that "We know, from our experience with changing from 6 to 5 days and back again that it is possible to get at least the same amount of production in five or more days than in six." Just like the eight-hour working day opened us up to greater prosperity, the five days of work will make it possible to enjoy even more success.

That company was one among the most profitable of the mid-twentieth-century, and the man in charge is still considered one of America's greatest executives. Henry Ford was his real name.

This anecdote shows us that working longer hours does not make you more productive.

Systems and a holistic approach to work and life are essential for bringing happiness and satisfaction, which in turn will increase productivity. However, there are many hacks and tricks to help increase our efficiency. These simple steps can prove to be extremely effective when implemented. These are some of the top tips.

1. Schedule Breaks

Working less hours is the smartest way to increase energy and productivity. Like every muscle in the body, the brain is a muscle. Regular stress wears it down. In order to recharge the brain's performance, it needs to be taken off-duty between work hours. This is something that everyone believes, but the data was lacking. It was confirmed by research that recommends 17 minutes for the ideal break. This is based on the experiment performed by 'DeskTime.

Ergonomics Research Laboratory employed a computer program to remind workers to take longer breaks in 1999. Workers who were reminded to take the break were on average 13% more productive than those who did not. This experiment was intended to analyze the behaviors of its most productive workers. The top ten per cent of employees were those who worked for 52-minutes, then took 17-minute breaks from the screen. This experiment reinforced the idea that productivity can be increased by taking short breaks.

2. Buffer Period

It is important that you allow room for unexpected events in your schedule. It is a good idea not to overload your calendar with work. You should allow yourself some buffer time to unwind and reorient. You can also use this time to envision and plan the way you'll tackle the task.

A meeting that takes place between 11 a.m. and 11:45 a.m. should be held immediately after your work hours of 10:50 to 10 a.m. You'll be more productive and have better clarity. Or, you might just take a break to allow your brain to rest and improve productivity. Here, a five-minute meditation is enough.

3. Willpower

Gary Keller said that willpower is not at one's will. He explained how willpower's peak and lowest points are during the day. To stay on top and do the important work necessary to align with the long term agenda, we must make use of all the willpower that is available.

He used the example of research in which every time a decision has been made, the blood sugar level drops in our bodies. As we get older, we fall prey to the temptation of doing easy work instead of the important things. He concluded that it is wise not to lose sight of your willpower, even if it isn't available.

Mornings are best for the most important work. you may do deep work. It is better to eat food with a lower glucose index than junk food in order to maintain constant sugar levels.

4. Habits

"Motivation and habit are what get you started. It is what keeps you going." -Jim Ryun.

Depending on your current system and your personal preferences, this book can make a significant impact on your life. You might be an absolute beginner or an expert trying to perfect your Task Management skills.

You might be inspired to make your productivity a priority after reading this book. Like previous attempts, however, life is going to take over soon and they will fall back into old habits. It is easy to retreat into their comfort zone.

This vicious cycle can be broken by discipline, but it's not enough to create a habit. While a habit is difficult to form, it can be formed and maintained without much effort. It is possible to find lots of information about habit formation. Some claim that it takes 21 to 3 weeks to create a new routine. Research has shown that it takes 66 days to develop a new habit, and then integrate it into your subconscious. This is why you should stick to the plan for 66 consecutive days. If you feel like quitting, then just keep going and enjoy an organized, productive, happy life.

5. Monotasking

Research found that only 2.5% have the ability to multitask. You might think you can multitask but your brains are not capable of simultaneously focusing on many things.

Multi-tasking makes us dopamine addicts, much like drug addiction. When we perform little tasks, our brain stimulates us with a little dopamine, the pleasure neurochemical, whenever we do them. This was a stimulant for our ancestors who were motivated to get things done. These small pleasures neurochemical can be found in answering emails and responding to tweets.

In 1950s America, rats were allowed to press a button that releases dopamine. They did this until everything was gone, even eating and drinking. Dopamine became more important to them than food and they ended up dying from starvation.

It is up to us to improve our own skills. We need to make sure we don't get distracted by things that do not make us productive. It may be a genuine addiction or chemical addiction.

Paolo Cardini, designer and educator said, "Forget multitasking. Try monotasking." This simple change will help you to be more efficient and productive as you won't have to focus on multiple tasks at once. This simple change makes it easier to be more efficient and effective. You won't lose your focus or feel overwhelmed by information.

6. Regular review

To keep machinery running smoothly, it is important to perform routine maintenance. The same goes for to do lists. Life will bring you many tasks every day. To keep up with them all, you'll need to regularly update your task management software. Each year, set some goals. You can use your months, week, and days as a way to get to the final goal. The task system should include regular planning sessions and system-evaluation to avoid getting caught in a wasteful process. Monthly, semi-annual and annual revisions are necessary to remove inefficiencies and confirm you're moving in the direction that you want.

Every day spend five minutes reviewing how much work you've done. You can adjust the weekly schedule to include any item that is not being completed in order to meet your monthly goal.

Every day counts. Take care of you and your days.

Chapter 9: Pen-&-Paper Versus Digital List

"People don't take anything seriously until it's written down, and then it becomes a daily part of their schedule." While it will take time to master, once you do, you'll be able to make all your plans a part of your daily routine.

People who enjoy making lists can be divided into two groups based upon their love for digital and tangible lists.

Many factors come into play when choosing a preferred method. Some people prefer to stick to the basics and keep a to-do checklist. They have a good reason for being so. Research shows that writing with your fingers creates a brain/hand link. We learn more and retain more. The pure joy of checking things off the list is irresistible. This dopamine rush seems to be worth the effort. You can get the same benefits from writing it down that you cannot with typing.

However, typing it and naming it then filing it later can prove tedious. Today's world is full of so many tasks that it can get overwhelming. It could be that a meeting has been cancelled or that plans have changed at last-minute. It is easier to make changes to your calendar and to-dolist app than to completely change your list. Separate lists for home and work are necessary. A digital schedule will allow you to be more mobile.

It is interesting that Professor at McGill University Daniel Levitin's preferred method for making a list is not an app. He gave very simple, low-tech tips for maintaining your To-Do List. He used 3X5 index cards to write down his tasks. It allows him to reorganize, reprioritize and so on. Focus on one task at a time and you won't be distracted by email notifications or emails.

It is logical, because your computer isn't associated with your To-Do List. However, you do most of your tasks there. The brain associates the activity and focus when the object is tangible, like a pen, paper list, a notebook, or index card. It doesn't matter which one you use, as long it is physical and in a space. A computer can be associated with many different activities. This is a difficult task for the brain.

Barbara Corcoran is the same as Dr. Daniel in her views regarding her to do list. Her words are, "I see my daily list of to-dos as the real deal in my life and treat it with respect." Even though I've tried various online to-dos lists, I simply cannot keep a to-do checklist that isn't written down or typed. I find the joy in crossing off tasks from a list with the delete button frustrating, so I always write them down.

Many people praised pen and paper lists during the interviews. Notepads, pens or paper are all good options for these people. Suzanne R. said, "Paper & pen work best" in the end. There are many apps out there, like Outlook, OneNote or Evernote. None of them are as accessible and usable as a paper notepad.

The number of people who prefer digital lists is increasing for simplicity's sake. One can easily connect their devices to their preferred apps or calendar. You won't forget to take lists with you. It is also more efficient if one considers how much time one loses if one must rewrite the entire list just to add or shuffle items in the schedule. Rita M., a colleague, shared her opinion that Outlook tasks are useful for tracking deadlines, particularly future ones. "It's more fun to cross things off a list than using Outlook Tasks to do this."

Some are trying hybrid. They are able to have the best of both technology and crossing.

They have chosen to use a combination of both even though it might seem difficult to some.

Natasha S. chooses the system that suits her best. She explained that she uses both an online and a paper calendar to keep track of her tasks and to-dos. She divides them into A, B, and C. When a task has been completed, she places it beside it. When it is canceled she places an "X" beside it. When it is pending she places a bullet beside it. And if the task is being moved forward she places forward arrows beside it. She said it was a leftover from her experience with Day-Timer and Franklin Covey. She said that you should sync your paper calendar and your online calendar. Natasha acknowledged that it could seem overwhelming, and she said that "This works well for me, but may be too overwhelming for others."

It's possible to organize your tasks and get a printed copy of your daily calendar.

It is important not to get too caught up in methodology. This guide is designed to help you form your formula. Make sure it is suited to your life and your schedule. Maybe you already have a preference, but if not, you can take a week and see what works. Some days you can be totally techy while others you can keep your handwritten list and cross off the tasks manually. Test it by combining the two. To live stress-free, find what suits you best and stick with it.

What Are You Looking To Achieve With Your Life?

There are things you should do before you can design your ideal workflow calendar. First, determine the end result you're looking for.

Two important things will result from taking the time to answer this question:

1) Your answers will allow you to delegate tasks or eliminate those that don't support your goals.

2) You will be motivated to achieve your goals.

This is why this question is important. Because there are many distractions and tasks competing to your attention. It's easy get distracted by emails, meetings, or admin tasks and lose sight of what really matters.

There is plenty of information on goal setting. It doesn't matter what you do, but it is important to have a clear picture of your goals and to keep it in sight. Then compare each task with it. Before you can commit to any task, you need to understand the reasons behind it. Which of your goals is the task in alignment with?

The best way to begin is to imagine your ideal workweek.

* Are you a freelancer? It is possible that you will spend most of your day completing and delivering work. Time is needed to communicate with clients, invoicing and communicating with them. It is important to increase your client base and promote yourself by offering quotes on new work.

* Are employees a possibility? You will spend most of your time doing assigned work. Also, you'll need time to meet with new leads and perform administrative tasks.

* Do you split your work time between raising children, running a household, or working? Your work week will contain a delicate

balance of your family life, your children's commitments and your work tasks.

Everybody's job and life is different. Your ideal workweek will not be the same as anyone else's. But I guarantee that your ideal work week doesn't include hours spent looking through old emails or on social media.

Let's use an example. The ideal work week for a freelance writer is the one below:

* 60% client work

* 20% client acquisition

* 10% Communication with existing clients

* 10% administrative and/or financial tasks

You're behind on a deadline on a project. You still have one hour to complete the project and there are two other items on your to-do list. What can you do?

1) Prepare a complex and lengthy application for an exciting project.

2) Keep your social media accounts updated with the latest projects you have completed and leave comments on related posts.

The social media task can be the most rewarding and easy of the two. But what are your goals? To help you decide which social media admin tasks will be the best for your day, consider your ideal week. Ask yourself why you would want either one of these tasks completed. It's simpler, or it aligns more closely with your goals.

You can make your choice. Although project applications are more difficult than other tasks, they can be rewarding. The project application is included in the 20% time allowed for new client acquisition. Social media updates can be included in the 10% that is allowed for administrative and financial tasks. Your career depends on how well you bring in clients and project proposals. It is the project application that makes you the best choice.

These decisions will help you prioritise your time, and plan your day. You will be able to make better decisions.

* Have you set your goals?

* Know your goals

* Learn how your ideal workweek looks.

Your To Do list will never be finished

Be aware that your to-do lists will never be finished. There will always be more tasks on your to-do list. Sometimes, the number added tasks is greater than what you complete each day. Your goal should not be to cross off every item on the to-do list. It is impossible.

This is what distinguishes to-do list from other types.

Planning an event? You may create a list listing all the tasks you will need to complete in order for it to be a success. It is important to complete these tasks before your event. Similar rules apply to a shopping or vacation packing list.

Your to do list is a unique representation of your life. It describes your daily routine and prioritizes how you use your time. This is your job description. It's your list of responsibilities.

Are you willing to go through every item on your to-do list? What would you do?

After crossing off items throughout the day, it's normal to feel disappointed when our list doesn't exist anymore. We grumble as we add items.

It is crucial to recognize that your to-do-list will never be finished and will always grow.

Now you can:

* Get rid of the false impression that the list will soon disappear

* Stop treating each item equal

* Prioritize your priorities and make the most of your time.

Productivity or the Feeling Of Productivity?

It's easy to fall in this trap. It's easy to fall into this trap. This idea is related to the earlier idea of goal setting and knowing what you want.

Let's look at the freelance writer with only one hour. You could apply to a new job that, if you were successful, would generate six months' work. However, this could be an argument for not doing it:

* The full hour will be taken

* Provide detailed information about your education and work experience.

* You may not be offered any job or receive acknowledgement.

In this view, there's no reason to delay the application.

Yet, 20% of your ideal workweek was dedicated to new client acquisition. You did this because you had to. Let's reexamine those arguments:

* "The application will require the entire hour." - That time could be used for work. It is better to save it than waste it. Success as a freelancer is dependent on bringing in new clients and new projects.

* "The application asks you to give specific answers about your qualifications. - Although you may not be granted the project, your application will help you apply to future ones.

* "You may not receive any new work or an acknowledgment of your request." - Although there's always the chance of your application being rejected, you won't be offered any new work.

Although it may not be exciting to create the application, you know that being a freelancer is essential for your success.

You could also spend that hour looking through your inbox. You are busy with client projects, and you have 200+ emails that need your attention. In that time, you can delete spam, ads, as well as newsletters. You could make notes of your upcoming appointments, and then reply to the simplest emails. An hour later, you'd have less 20 critical emails to which you'll create detailed replies.

How would you feel if your inbox was reduced from 200 to 20 in the short term?

* You'd experience a tremendous sense of short term satisfaction.

* You would feel more productive and busy.

* Anybody could ask you how your last hour was spent at work.

These feelings can be very tempting. Understanding this important truth is crucial.

Tasks that give you a short-term feeling like productivity are often not those that get us closer towards our goals.

The same applies to meetings. Many of the most powerful and successful people on the planet say no to even the most critical meetings. When they do agree to attend a meeting they usually set a strict time limit.

They'll only accept to attend when the organiser has reduced their agenda and written a goal.

Successful people understand that meetings can make you feel busy and important. But meetings are not always productive.

Learn to recognize the differences between

* A short-term sense of productivity.

* The discomfort that can often accompany tasks that lead to our desired goals.

Instead of focusing solely on what you feel during the task at hand, take a look ahead at how your day will be when you evaluate it.

This is how it would look. It's the freelance writer. It's the last day of the workday, and you are still thinking about your day.

* How would it feel to choose to spend the last hour of your day sorting through emails? The rush and busyness you felt that day would long be gone. It's still on your to-do

lists. It'd be regrettable if you didn't complete it.

* How would it feel to spend an hour applying for a job? The hard work and short-term discomfort would soon be forgotten. You'd feel that you made the best of your short working hours and finished your day feeling high.

Science: Why Lists Are Failing

To do lists can be used as a way to organize your tasks. Your success with a to-do list depends on how well you set it up, and how often you use it. It is unlikely that your to-do-list will ever complete the tasks you have set. Even if you have a well-organized to-do list, it won't be used.

Even the best to-do list may not be enough to make it easy to accomplish your tasks and still be productive. We won't go into science or psychology to explain these reasons. Let's focus on the reasons that a to do-list can hinder productivity.

* Feeling overwhelmed seeing all the tasks on your to-do lists.

* A feeling that you will never complete all the items no matter how hard or fast you try. This is due to the false belief that we should try to complete every item on our list.

* Lack of prioritizing, which leads you to regard basic administrative tasks as equally important as major projects. This causes you to spend too much time on mundane tasks in order to get them done. You are neglecting critical tasks.

* Feeling lost or confused by having different tasks in your life. Confusion can lead to overwhelm when you have home chores.

* Overwhelm and disappointment when you add new products faster than you get to check off your completed items.

To-do lists often fail because they do not represent the tasks that you have to complete at a particular moment. As you will quickly discover, a calendar solves the problem. A calendar depicts the passing of time as a fluid concept. It is natural to add new items on a calendar, as you are able to experience every day in a continuous fashion. A calendar doesn't have a beginning nor an end. This captures time's inevitability. It is possible to use lists to represent a subset, or a set of tasks that will eventually come to an end. Examples of great lists include a shopping checklist or a list with tasks to plan an occasion. Each one of these lists must have a clear end. It makes sense that you should aim to complete each of these lists.

Later in this book we will examine the benefits of using calendars instead of to-do lists in more detail.

Urgent Versus Important

To-do lists are still useful for many people. However, it is crucial to recognize the difference between important or urgent items. Do you really want other people's priorities to override yours?

Let's suppose you get an email form a colleague. The colleague has dropped the ball in a project and needs data from you to complete their report. Meanwhile, your project is on hold for several weeks. You've been working hard on it every day to ensure that your best work is produced.

It's easy to react, but it can also be tempting to jump in and do the right thing when the task is urgent. You must respond to your colleague's urgent email as they have very specific time requirements. It is important to know the difference between important and urgent. Although your own project may not seem urgent at this time, it is still important.

What would it look like if you dropped your work to help a coworker meet their deadline? You'll feel important and busy at the same time. Later in the day you would regret that you did not make progress on your important task. Instead, you dealt with the urgent task of another person. Your colleague made it sound like their work was very important, but it was really only urgent. It did not help you achieve your goals.

Most emails that you receive concern urgent tasks. Your tasks may not be as important as they seem to others, but people try their best. You will only be able to see a small percentage of the tasks as important. It can be tempting just to respond to urgent or time-sensitive tasks. It will make it impossible to complete important tasks on your own.

This is the number one reason people fail in achieving their personal goals. This is why it's important to have a goal, such as learning a language or writing a book. But, it is not enough to compete with the flood of urgent tasks.

You will fail if you don't distinguish between urgent and more important causes. This distinction makes relying on a planner far more productive. You can use a calendar system to assign non-negotiable tasks priority. Your day will no longer be spent putting out others' fires.

The importance of saying "No!"

If you look closely at the habits and behaviors of successful people, there are many common themes. One is that they are able to say "No!" to almost everything. This is how you distinguish between important and urgent tasks. You are responsible for important tasks, such as long-term goals and projects. Urgent tasks often benefit someone else.

You can think back to the colleague who requested data from you in order to finish their own project. You were not the only one who was interested in this project. Your colleague presented the project as urgent and tried to pass it on.

This book has been written for you because you are having trouble managing your to-do lists. You're searching for a better approach to managing your increasing number of tasks. We have talked about prioritizing so that the easier tasks don't take precedence over the more difficult ones. We discussed not letting other people's priorities take precedence over your important tasks.

It is important to say "No" at a higher level. You won't be able say "No" to your employer if they assign you a task. This holds true regardless of whether the task falls within the "urgent" category at the expense or priority of other tasks. As an employee, you have some responsibilities. You are expected to do the job assigned. You risk losing your job if this is not done. Don't these tasks now have a higher level of importance?

You might be able to say "No!" to projects that aren't in line with your goals as a freelancer/consultant. You will eventually have to accept a decent salary and be able to pay your bills.

The more powerful an individual is, the more free they are to pick and choose which agreement to. Everybody still has the freedom to say "No". This is applicable to students, entry-level workers, and freelancers starting out.

In the book we have already discussed:

* Understanding the goals you are trying to achieve

* Imagine what your ideal week of work looks like

* Allocating a percentage to each component of your workweek.

This question should be asked whenever you get a request or an opportunity that you don't have the right to say no to. "How does this fit in my ideal workweek?"

While you may not have the freedom to say "No", to a new job project, For example, you might say "No!" to a request to have after-work drinks at a former coworker. It might be more productive to spend this time with friends and family, or exercise, or on long-term projects.

These kinds of choices can appear in tiny ways, such checking your email. Even though it appears like you're operating on autopilot all the time, you're constantly making choices.

* The ability to read a newsletter, or a catalogue

* Answering a questionnaire

* Clicking an ad by a retailer you've previously bought from

* Watching a YouTube Video or reading an article that was sent by a friend.

You always have the option to say "No" in such situations. Simply delete the email and move onto the next. To avoid being forced to do the same thing again, you can click "Unsubscribe".

As you gain more success, more people will want your time and attention. People will be interested in you as a mentor, collaborator, or interviewer. You only have so much time in a day, and you have so few days. You should not give up your time. Your goal is to get there first, so you can say yes to the people and places that are most exciting.

Successful people rely on their calendars

Before I started writing the first word of this book, I spent months conducting extensive research. I was interested in how people kept their to-dos lists. I found that most people struggle to keep a detailed and useful to-do list. I saw people feeling overwhelmed and frustrated with their to do lists. I knew there had to be "to-do lists that worked", hence the title of this book, which is used by the most successful people around the globe.

I didn't wish to invent the wheel, or develop yet another to-do list method or app. Instead, I set out to discover the patterns of success.

I believe that the best and most productive people on the planet use a different version of the to-do list. That system was what I wanted to simplify for everyone.

The unexpected result made me question if I should write a new book title. I was correct in stating that the most successful people on the planet use a similar system. They used this method to keep themselves organized and on top for their tasks over the course of each day, week and month. My surprise was that they were not using a list.

Successful people do not write to do lists. Successful people use their calendars to plan their work. But success is not about work. People who are successful live and work off their calendars.

Why did you choose "To Do Lists THAT Work" for the book's title? Because I know how many people are suffering around the world.

* Bouncing between one to do and the next method

* Watching them become more frustrated as their to-do-lists grow

* Never feeling at the top of their job.

Tired of trying so hard to manage their overwhelming and confusing to-do list.

People want a to do list system that works.

Here it is. However, it's actually not a to-do list.

A list of all the things that must be done is not how successful people work. The calendar helps them break down their days into 15-minute periods.

The most productive, successful and productive people in the world schedule everything. They all believe the same thing, no matter how they realize it.

"If it'sn't on the calendar it won't get done."

Here are some things you can expect to see in the remainder of this book, after the foundation ideas have been discussed.

* How you can turn your to-do list in to the calendar system used to make the most of life.

* Maintaining the best possible calendar system for you.

* Case studies that show how different people have made the transition to the calendar system.

Step-By Step Method to Create To-Do Lists That Work

One-time steps

You must first implement a calendar system to reap its benefits. First, you will need to move from your current to-do lists to the calendar.

Here's the good stuff:

* You just need to follow these steps.

* Only one step is required.

Let's get started!

Write your Goal/Mission Statement

Let's look at the bigger picture. Before you can begin to block out time on your calendar, you should have a goal or mission statement. This will be the standard against which you judge each task.

Your time is limited. It is impossible to put something on your calendar without taking the test. The test will teach you how to ask:

* Why is the task so important?

* What am I doing it to?

* Why does it merit a spot on my calendar

* Why should a significant amount of my time be sacrificed for this?

These questions can be answered quickly with your goal or mission statements.

Do you have a mission or a goal already? You can revise your mission statement and goal again.

If you don't have a mission statement or a goal, now is the perfect time to make one.

This book does not address goal setting. I am not trying to recapitulate the much larger work of other authors on the topic. The best way to develop your mission statement is by reading books about goal setting. Stephen R. Covey has written several books on the topic.

It is possible to quickly create a mission-statement using an online tool. I recommend Stephen Covey's free tool https://msb.franklincovey.com/. It's easy to find similar tools online by performing a quick Google search.

A mission statement or goal does not have to be complex. This step is important. You don't need a mission statement. Write one down.

Your mission statement is simply your "why". It is the standard against whom you will measure the value of your tasks in order to decide if they are worthwhile.

While it is vital to establish a goal or mission statement in this stage, it doesn't need be complicated.

Let's now turn our attention to the first case study. Charlie agreed to go through the steps of the book and record their progress. These steps are clearly visible when you watch

Charlie change from a to-do to list to a planner.

Charlie, 31, parent/freelancer

In My Own Words

"I'm single with two school-age children. I am a freelance graphics designer. I have full custody of my kids so I can only work during school. It depends on what we are doing, but sometimes I can squeeze in a couple hours on weekends. Freelancing fits my life because I can work from home and make my own hours. I put my family first, and I'm there for them even if that means less work week.

Current To Do List

"It's more chaotic than anything!" I keep all of the children's classes and appointments on my calendar. But, I tend not to keep much of my client work in my mind. I've tried to note down due dates and other deadlines, but my list never seems complete so it's not something I rely upon.

I can visualize where all my projects stand and when they are due. Sometimes, this can mean that I wake up in panic because I haven't remembered something due. I'm aware I need to be organized and have better systems for tracking everything.

Sometimes I become overwhelmed with the limited amount of time I have to work and end up doing everything I can to make myself miserable. I'll spend an entire hour on social media scrolling or doing housework to ruin my day.

Write your mission/goal statement

"To be the best mother I can be and to always be there when my children need me. To be as smart and efficient as I can while working, but not to let my work take over time with my family. I will see them grow up quickly and I want to make sure they have the best time possible.

I love to grow my logo design business. It's fine to do basic graphic design tasks. But, I want to become an expert at designing logos. I would like to decrease the time spent on other projects. Soon, I'll be completely focused on logo design and won't take any other projects. I'll be a one stop shop for any company that needs the perfect logo.

Find your not-negotiables

All highly successful people adhere to a set of essentials. The majority of successful people do not work all hours. Instead, they have a set of strict working hours. People who are successful have strict time and travel restrictions. It's not unusual for CEOs to always be home at the right time to eat dinner or for their children to attend weekend sports events. Succession is also a priority for successful people. They know how many hours are necessary to perform at their peak.

Now it is time to decide on your non-negotiables. At this point, you won't be putting anything on your calendar - instead, you will be writing a checklist.

Consider these examples as examples, and then add other ones as needed.

Sleep

How many hours sleep do you require to function at your best?

You might not remember how refreshing it feels to wake up fresh if you have been sleeping too late or getting up too early.

If you are unsure, try starting with seven or eight hours. Then experiment over several weeks. Soon you'll find the amount of sleep you need to feel awake without feeling dizzy.

The time you go back to sleep and when you wake from sleep are also important. Your sleep health will depend on the amount of sleep that you get and how long you stay asleep. You can sleep eight hours from 3 a.m. up to 11 a.m., but not eight hours from 10:00 to 6:00 a.m.

If you aren't sure what your ideal sleep pattern is, take a chance and start to experiment in the next few weeks.

Hours of operation

Work, sleep, repeat. Sometimes it seems like you spend all of your time following this routine. It's time to set clear boundaries about your working hours.

As mentioned, successful people keep strict working hours. They know that they must work within their schedules.

Parkinson's Law, a work of C. Northcote Parkinson, is something you may have heard.

"Work expands in order to fill the time it takes to complete."

So if you have an hour for a task to complete, you will most likely complete it in that hour. If you were given a three-week deadline for the same task, it would take you three weeks to complete it.

Although it might seem counterintuitive at first, having set work hours can make you more productive. Being able to know when you will finish your work at a specific time will help you be more productive.

There will always remain more work. Setting realistic goals and sticking to it will allow you to achieve your daily tasks.

Exercise

Exercise is often forgotten about when things get too busy. You should make exercising a top priority.

Write down when, how often and for how much exercise you plan to do. You can write down whether you are doing regular yoga or spinning classes, how many days per week, or running every morning.

Partner

You're probably in a relationship and you know how important scheduling time for your spouse is. While a weekly date evening sounds wonderful in theory, it is unlikely to happen if both of you make it a priority.

Children

As a parent, it is easy to forget how precious these years are. You'll soon find your children no longer want to be with you, and will instead chase them.

The relationship you desire to build with your kids is what you should be thinking about. What does this look and feel like every day?

* Do you want them to come to school each morning?

* Should evening meals be shared?

* Will your commitment be to helping with homework?

Consider what promises you would like to make to your kids. Now convert this into actual days and hours and write it all down.

Family and Friends

Too many people are unhappy about the loss of once-valuable friendships. This usually happens because one or the other of you didn't make an effort. You might have family members you wish that you put more effort into.

If guilt is a feeling, remember that it's the simplest tasks that you can push from one day onto the next.

* A weekly call to your parents

* A monthly visit to your aunts and uncles

* Send a message to your grandparents.

* Replying in an email or to a letter with news from your home

These are all tasks that you have to prioritize.

Meals

Have you ever:

* You drank coffee for breakfast when you were tired from staying up all night.

* For the sake of completing a project within a deadline, you skipped lunch.

* Had to make do with a handful of biscuits and a muesli-bar for lunch, as you had back-toback meetings.

If you don't nourish yourself, your brain function and energy levels as well as your mood will suffer. You should consider the most effective meal schedule for you. Then, write down the time and duration.

Self-Care

What gives you the most relaxation? What makes your soul feel rejuvenated? What are you most looking forward to in the future?

* A relaxing bubble bath that is free from interruptions

* Time for breakfast newspaper reading

* A weekly masseuse

* Sunday Golf

* Monthly Hair appointment

* Read in peace for thirty minutes before bed.

Write down your self-care philosophy.

Work-Specific

Depending on the circumstances of your job, there may be work-specific items that you cannot agree to.

* Do you value a phone call or meeting every day if you are a manager or mentor of mentees?

* Do you find it helps to read the latest journal articles?

Be aware that we are talking about tasks that align well with your goals and values at this stage. These tasks are not obligatory. We'll get there later.

Long-Term goals

Your long-term goals could be personal or work-related.

* Have you ever promised yourself that you would learn to play the electric guitar, but

have never been able to get the time or the motivation to practice?

* Do your weekly self-criticisms include: Did you spend too much time writing or editing your memoir?

* Your crafting supplies are gathering dust despite your promise to yourself that you'd make time for it?

Write down any long-term goal or passion you have.

* How often do you plan to work on it each week? One week? Every day?

* How many sessions should you have and at what hour is it best to do them? The best time to start is when you have the entire house to yourselves. Sunday evenings where everyone else is relaxing by the TV.

Charlie, 31, parent/freelancer

Find your not-negotiables

Sleep

"7 hours from 10:00 pm. to 5:00 am. This allows me to have a couple hours alone after the kids go to bed. I will also have approximately an hour to get ready before I start helping my children get ready for school.

Working Hours

"9:00 to 2:45 p.m. every school day."

Exercise

"Spin class Tuesdays and Thursdays, 6:00 p.m. - 7:00. The creche is open to children.

Children

"My number 1 priority. "My number one priority.

Family and Friends

"I am going to try harder to catch up with high school friends and parents who are part of the baby group. Every Sunday morning, I'll make it down to the coffee house near the beach and stay for a while. I'll have breakfast for the kids while they play on my playground.

I'll let everyone know this is where I'll go every week. Anyone can come join me if they like, even if they don't have children. This could also be a great way to allow the kids to play with other children from school.

Meals

"Breakfast & dinner are already part and parcel of our daily lives. I sometimes skip lunch because of the rush to get things done during school hours. I'll make sure to cook an extra portion of dinner in order to have a meal ready for lunch the next morning.

Self-Care

"I read every night at bedtime, and I'll continue to do so." I'll read for 30 minutes, even if I'm usually awake 10 or 15 minutes later than I started.

This is the basic outline of your Calendar

It's now time to make your new calendar with the information you've already compiled. Below is a guideline for you: It can be used digitally or on paper. It is important to choose one that breaks down your day into 15 minute intervals.

It doesn't matter if you use a paper or digital planner, it is fine to continue using it. Your new system will be more effective if you have a familiar template. Use this template instead to create your schedule in a word document or spreadsheet.

Once you have drawn your outline, block in

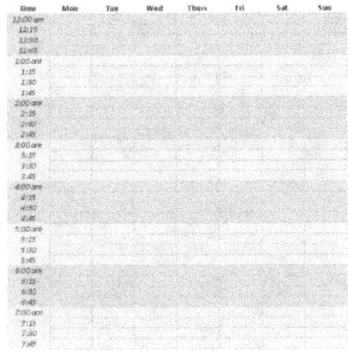

the non negotiables.

Charlie, 31, parent/freelancer

Josh, 19, student

Josh is the next case study. He is a student at University. Josh used this method to plan his calendar and prioritize.

In My Own Words

"I'm 19 years old, and I'm in my 2nd year of university. I'm studying law. I was able to manage decent results last school year, but now it is time to get organised. I'm currently working as a casual worker in a cafe. In addition to seeing my family and high school friends I like, I also enjoy time with my uni classmates.

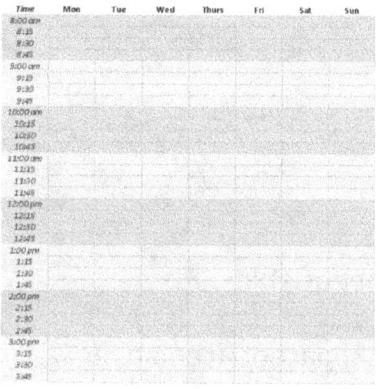

Current To Do List

To be completely honest, I don't really have a task list. I have my uni calendar and a list with due dates and deadlines for assignments. Each week, the cafe roster changes. I don't know what week's roster is until Saturday.

My main problem is getting started on assignments early so I can study for tests and exams. I find it difficult to get everything done on time.

Write your Goal/Mission Statement

"To take advantage of the opportunity and not waste my education. It's not enough just to get decent results and scrape by. "I want to know that my marks are representative of who I am."

Find your not-negotiables

Sleep

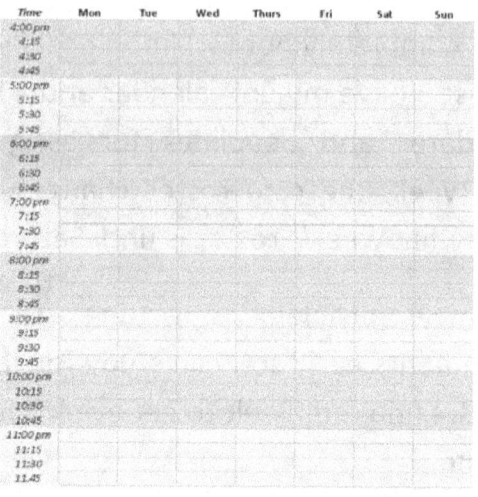

"I'm someone who needs eight hours a day minimum. Planning is key to ensure that I get enough sleep, especially on the mornings when I have classes. It's okay for me to stay up until midnight if I can go to bed early in the morning. But, I must stop staying up late until 2:00 AM and expect to be on my best behavior at 9:00 AM. lecture."

Working hours

My contact hours (lectures/tutorials, and labs), will be set at the beginning of each semester. Although my hours at the cafe may change each week due to the fact that it's open every night of the week, they are almost always open one day on weekends.

Family and Friends

"I'm trying to manage two different groups for the very first time. It is becoming difficult.

Time	Mon	Tue	Wed	Thurs	Fri	Sat	Sun
5:00 am 5:15 5:30 5:45	Wake up, shower, get ready	Wake up, shower, get ready	Wake up, shower, get ready	Wake up, shower, get ready	Wake up, shower, get ready	Wake up, shower, get ready	Wake up, shower, get ready
6:00 am 6:15 6:30 6:45 7:00 am 7:15 7:30 7:45	Breakfast together, get kids ready for school	Breakfast together, get kids ready for school	Breakfast together, get kids ready for school	Breakfast together, get kids ready for school	Breakfast together, get kids ready for school		Get kids up and ready
8:00 am 8:15 8:30 8:45	School drop off	School drop off	School drop off	School drop off	School drop off		Breakfast and catch-up at coffee shop
9:00 am 9:15 9:30 9:45						Family free time	
10:00 am 10:15 10:30 10:45	Work	Work	Work	Work	Work		
11:00 am 11:15 11:30 11:45							Family free time
12:00 pm 12:15 12:30 12:45	Lunch	Lunch	Lunch	Lunch	Lunch		

I don't wish to lose touch or get disconnected with my high school friends. However, I do want to spend quality time with my new friends at uni. I want to spend time with my family and my little brothers. Since I moved away, they have missed me.

Long-Term goals

"I promised myself that when I left home, I would begin working on screenplays. I am well into my 2nd year and have yet to start. It is clear that I won't be able to take any more time after I finish my uni and start working as an attorney. If I pass up this opportunity, I'll regret it."

Notes about Calendar Blocking

"My schedule changes weekly as a result of the cafe roster and daily as a result of my uni timestamp. This chaos messes with my head. It would be great if I could set a timetable.

For example, on three days per week, my earliest contact time is a 9-o'clock lecture. Even though my day starts later on the second and third days, I should treat all days as if they were 9 o'clock in the morning. I should devote that time studying and doing assignments.

It is important to view my study as a job. I must not only attend lectures every hour, but also treat it as a full-time job. Remember that we were told to expect three- or four hours of studying for each hour of contact.

The same goes for my work schedule. I usually work three nights a semaine, between 5:00 p.m. and 8:00.

This should be added to my calendar just like I would if it were Monday through Friday. When I'm off work, I can do other things, like catch up with my family. My parents and brothers would love to invite me over for dinner two times a week. I'm sure they won't mind that the nights are different each week.

Reveal Your Current To Do Liste

Your not-negotiables are now in place. Now you have the basic outline for your calendar. Well done! Now, it's time to get into the details. Now, break down the bigger blocks that were previously assigned to broad topics, such as "work".

Make a list of your current tasks, or a pile of them if there are more. You can write down tasks that you have completed without notifying the owner. To do lists might not include things like checking emails or sending texts.

If you don't work with a list currently, make a note of everything.

You will need to create a heading that describes each block of time you have in your calendar. We'll start by addressing the major block of time, which is work. This process can then be repeated for other large blocks of time, such as "exercise", free time, or family time. In some cases, all you need is to finish the work section. It all depends on your current to-do lists system.

Are there personal tasks on your to-dos list like washing dishes, cleaning up after pets, and paying bills? If so, continue the same steps to improve your home life after you have finished the work sections.

Let's start by listing your tasks for work. You can start by making a list. You can then add any tasks, such as checking your emails, that you don't need to be prompted. Ask yourself:

* What tasks should I complete each day?

* How can I spend my time working?

You must be honest with yourself. It is your benefit and your boss/clients will never see your lists. It's okay to include tasks you aren't supposed to spend time on, but you need to.

* Checking out social media

* Making personal calls

* Playing mobile games

Do you feel stuck or unsure of what you do in your working hours? Your email inbox could be your makeshift to-do list, or it could be that you're running on autopilot. Take a moment to write your list.

Write down all your activities during the next week. It doesn't matter if you write it down every time. Don't worry if you have already written "Check email" once you do it.

In no time, you'll have a workable list. This is your task: Divide the list into two parts: one-off and repeating tasks.

* Repeating tasks can be things you do everyday or several times per day like checking your email.

* This includes writing a report or sending a specific message via email or making a telephone call.

You will need to add your repeating tasks in your calendar. These tasks will be completed in your calendar. You will have a separate list for your one-off tasks to help you prioritize and keep track.

Now, continue working on your work list. Split your task list into repeating tasks or one-off tasks.

You might be surprised to see that not all the items in this list fall within either category.

* The name of the book recommended by a friend

* A friend's b-day

* A motivational saying you loved so much you had it written down.

Anything that isn't a repeating or one-off task will get addressed in the next section.

Charlie, 31, parent/freelancer

Reveal Your Current To Do Liste

Work

Repeating tasks

* Send an email to find out anything important or brand new

* Read and delete any newsletters or other generic emails

* Reply business emails

* Reply personal emails

* Comment on the comments to check business social media accounts

* Write new social media posts

* Invoicing--create new invoices, verify old invoices for payment and send reminders

* Find freelancing opportunities, apply to new projects

* Update resumes and portfolios with recent projects

* Look for job postings and tender boards for big projects.

One-Off Tasks

* Second round to amend the logo for a coffee shop

* Sketch three homepage design suggestions for an ad agency

* Complete layout of law firm newsletter, and submit

* Continue to follow up with copywriter. Source stock images for future social media posts.

* Short photographer before next week's boutique photo shoot

Register Your "Notes for Self" List

Here's something uncomfortable about to do lists.

The majority of tasks listed in traditional to-do lists you will never complete are not completed. These tasks will not only be impossible to complete, but they will also not be started.

But people don't always realize that when they add an item on their to-do list. One would never write down a task for the purpose of never accomplishing it. Most people are simply too busy to complete these tasks.

* Watch this funny video sent by their high school friend

* Refer to the book recommended by their relative.

* Or check out prices for similar health insurance plans.

You should write these down, even though you won't be able to complete them. Why? Because it helps to write things down. This frees you up to do more important tasks.

Visualize your mind as a Ferris Wheel. Each compartment is home to something you are trying to recall:

* A quote you liked

* The weekend forecast

* A reminder that you need to purchase a birthday gift card

* The book idea you read in the shower.

All of these thoughts are constantly going around. Writing them down will help you feel more at peace and clear your mind. Now your brain can focus more on important tasks such as driving, and less on the same thoughts.

Later we'll be discussing the advantages of carrying a notebook (real or virtual) with you at all time. Now is the time to make a "Notes-to-Self" list. This list could be virtual or real.

You can use a Word or Excel file, or a Google Doc/Sheet that's cloud-based.

A virtual list allows you to group items together and move them around.

* All birthdays in one

* A comprehensive list of book recommendations.

* Other YouTube videos you should be watching every day

* All of your favourite motivational quotations in one place

If you prefer to work with pen & paper, this will also work.

A list of everything that you have on your current task list. This list can be either a repeating or one-off task. This is now called your "Notes to Self", or "Notes to Self" List. These notes and ideas are now your "Notes To Self" list. But they don't compete with actual tasks.

It's likely that you won't take any action on most of these items. But that's okay. It will only be possible to reference the list if it is necessary. Ask your friend, "What was the name for that book you told me about last year?" If you have a list of books, you can find the name from that list. There are many YouTube videos that you can look at when you have to commute long distances or wait in line at an airport.

Most importantly, your mind can concentrate on more important tasks. There's no need for your mind to be churning through the same list.

Charlie, 31, parent/freelancer

Register Your "Notes for Self" List

* Do a Udemy drawing course together with the kids - udemy.com/draw-cute-characters ?

* Mini notebook craft - https://youtu.be/Y-XcyV9rwwY

* Furry notebook DIY - https://www.youtube.com/watch?v=kLAdEgtgLQA

* "They may forget everything you said, but they'll never forget how you made 'em feel." - Carol Buchner

Start a Task List

Now it is time to take care of your one-off needs.

To keep track of your special tasks and give priority to them, create a new "Task List".

We're currently working within the "Work" block. This area will be the most important for most people. For another block of time on your calendar, you may find it useful to repeat the same steps.

* Enjoy a free time

* Exercise

* Study

* Working towards a certain goal.

We will now focus on your Work space. Everything that was previously a one-off task on your task list is going to be transferred to your new list. The following headings will be your starting point. You can change them as you need.

Assigned date - This is the date that you were assigned the task or project. It's not when you started working on it, but when it became your responsibility.

Due Date - This is the date you must finish the task. This may be:

* Set by your superiors/client

* Negotiated between yourself and the other party

* Assign the task by yourself, particularly if it is part of a larger job.

Description - Brief description or title of the task without going into detail.

Urgency - refers to someone else's priorities, not yours. "Urgent" tasks are those that someone else needs you to complete in order to get their work done. You might be impatient, or they may have put off assigning the task. The other party is the one who must act urgently, unless you were the one who forgot.

You can assign this task a score in this column based on how urgent it seems. You will get angry phone calls and emails if this task is not completed immediately. If we look at prioritizing our tasks, you will see that urgency is a factor to consider.

Importance is back in the spotlight. Which task is most important from your point of view? How important you view this task will depend on how you see it and the work you do.

* A task given by a long-term customer may be more important that a one-off job.

* A new client might assign you a task that may be more significant as you strive to impress and secure future work.

* A task that challenges your skills could be more important then busywork.

* A senior supervisor may assign a task that is more important than a regular task.

* Tasks that pay more may be considered more important than tasks with lower wages.

Alignment With Goals – Now, we'll return to your mission statement or goal. You may find a task urgent or important but it is not in alignment with the goals you have established.

Let's use an example. You are a freelancer and you have two roles.

* Legal transcription, where you can type out courtroom proceedings.

* Copywriting, where you create articles and website copy to help businesses.

Transcription pays the bills. It's a steady source for income. But it's not a fulfilling career. It's not your ideal career.

You wish to get rid of transcription and focus more time on copywriting. In the beginning of the book you mentioned that your goals were to:

* Develop your copywriting business

* You can take on more high-paying clients for copywriting

* Increase your copywriting skills while you reduce your transcription workload.

You are now given a new transcription task. Your client insists on the urgency of the task and is offering high rates of pay. It gets high marks in urgency and importance. The task isn't in line with your goals. The task should not be awarded a score of less than 0 in the Alignment with Goals column.

Fill out the table by adding your list of one-off jobs. Now, enter the items in any number you like. We will next prioritize your list.

Charlie, 31, parent/freelancer

Start a Task List

Prioritize Your Tasks

The next step in prioritising your task lists is to prioritize them. This is where your tasks will be listed in the order they are expected to be completed. Next, you can go through the list starting from the top.

An organized task list is invaluable. By prioritising your task list considering several variables, you're almost guaranteeing your success. Why? Why? Many feel guilt or panic when they make a mistake.

Is this something you've ever done? Then you realise that you have forgotten another task after spending all week working on it. The deadline for the second task has now been extended to an impossible length.

Prioritizing your tasks can make it easier to eliminate daily decision-making. Instead, you can start working, completing each task according to the order in which they are on your list.

Productivity experts are more likely to refer to your Most Important Task (or MIT). According to this theory, if your MIT is always known, you can focus solely on it. This is how you can ensure that your MIT is always in your mind. Even better, when you complete your MIT, your second task becomes your new MIT.

How do you prioritize your tasks then? Always consider the due dates column first. Late submissions and failure to keep promises is a serious offense. In rare cases, you might be allowed to submit late. Sometimes, you might be allowed to request an extension. However, this could cause you to lose your credibility and cause your clients/supervisors to seek out someone else.

A task may be important and aligned with goals. However, you must finish it before the due date.

It is important to order your tasks by due date.

It's easy to reorder your list if you work in a Microsoft Word document. If you prefer to use pen and ink, number each item. 1 is the top. Once you're done prioritising your list of items, rewrite it in its correct order.

If you don't know the due date of a task, it is a good idea for you to draft one.

* Is the task a part of a larger ongoing project or a smaller one? You should set a date so you have plenty of time to complete the next phase.

* Did someone assign you a task with no due date? The due date you believe your client/supervisor will follow up on you about this task is the basis for estimating it.

So that they aren't confused with official due dates, put estimated due dates in brackets.

Charlie, 31, parent/freelancer

Prioritize your Tasks

To Order Tasks By Due Date

Now, let's look at the third column - urgency and importance, as well as alignment with goals. Although there is no standard way to rank tasks on these columns, it is possible to use three scores to make sure you're not using the wrong formula.

* Do not confuse urgency or importance

* Prioritize tasks not aligning with your ultimate goals.

Once your task lists are finalized, you can put them aside. This list will soon be reviewed again.

Charlie, 31, parent/freelancer

Priority order of tasks

"I ordered the tasks by due dates and realized that I had 2 tasks due in 2 days that I had been neglecting. These tasks were very simple, like emailing or searching the internet. These two tasks could be completed in no more than 30 minutes. But they had been delayed for more than 2 weeks.

These are the tasks which would cause me to panic and realize I'd forgotten something. It is quite eye-opening seeing the tasks listed by due dates. It will only take about an hour to accomplish the first two tasks. I'll keep these two tasks at top of my newly prioritized task list.

"I still have three things to do.

* One is due by five days.

*The next due date is unknown, but I am estimating that the client will be following up with my about mid-February.

* The last one will not be due until another month.

I am now examining the importance and urgency columns. I have noticed that the law firm insists on me making their work a priority. I suppose that's the way many law firms work - they know what it takes to keep people on track.

It is also important to me that these tasks are in line with my goals.

Despite the fact that the law firm insists on their urgent work, it earns a 5 for its alignment with goals. I plan to concentrate on logo design, and not just graphic design.

There is no due date for the second round to amend the logo of the coffeeshop. The owner is very friendly and laid back and isn't as demanding than other clients. The logo work is exactly the kind of work I want, so I scored it 10. The client already indicated that I could use the finalized logo and other design ideas in my portfolio. I'll tackle this next task.

"The two remaining tasks each scored a 5-in alignment with goals column. One is due before the others." I will tackle them in this order.

Repetition Tasks can be batch-produced

It's now time to delete the list of repetitive tasks you have previously created. This section has the following purpose:

* Group your tasks together in a logical manner

* Put them on your calendar so you can do a variety of tasks at once.

If you're anything like most people you might do the same task repeatedly every day, sometimes without realising. You aren't sure if you fall into this category? You can keep track of the times that you check your phone, or your email every day.

Many people don't realize they are doing these tasks. Some people call it FOMO, or the fear that they will miss out on important emails or be out of touch. It can be a sign you are bored, or it could be a way to procrastinate and not tackle more important tasks. Whatever the reason it may be, it will eat into your productivity as well as your time. You might not even realize that it's happening.

You may have your email program set up to notify your when a message is added to your inbox. When you leave your desk, your phone is checking for new messages. Then you will check again on your computer when you return.

It is time to regain control and place limits on this unhealthy habit. It will feel strange at the beginning, and you may worry about missing something. It is normal for people to not expect an immediate response to emails. Although you might get a reply within 24hrs, this is not the same as receiving a reply that makes it impossible to check your email several times per minute. Even if you were on a flight or in a meeting you would not be able check your emails. There are no bad things that can happen in those few hours.

Check your repeating tasks list and note any items that have to do with emails. Consider the following:

* Check business email

* Check your personal email

* Take control of your inbox

* Reply to the most important email

* Take a look at newsletters and other FYI email types

All of these tasks can be combined.

Next, go into your settings and turn off email notifications. Although it is fine to keep your email account setup on your phone, you will need the preview popup to be disabled when a new message arrives. These distractions can pull you away from your task and distract your concentration.

Now you have a new repeating task: "Emails" which batch several tasks from your to-do list. Next, choose the best times to do this task. It's a good idea to schedule emails two to three times per day, depending on your needs. In those instances, you will be focusing on other tasks and won't check your email. While this will initially be painful and take some time to get used to, it'll pay off in the end.

You should also consider immediately responding to emails. If you do this, others will feel the need to immediately respond to your emails. This is especially true if you are their superior.

You can see it from their perspective. Imagine your boss sending a flood of emails to you every day. Imagine how difficult would it be to focus on a task assigned by your boss. If you felt guilty about not responding to your bosses emails, then you would prioritise replying even if it meant putting off your actual work. Other people can take a break from their email inboxes by waiting until your next email session.

You can group the items from your repeating task list together by looking at them. This will depend on the work you do and your personal circumstances. Examples include:

* Returning phone calls, including checking voice messages

* Make sure you set office hours that let your staff and coworkers know that you're available

* Financial, including checking bank account balances and paying invoices

* Invoicing, which includes creating new invoices or following up on any outstanding invoices

* Social media, including creating posts and replying on comments and messages

* Applying for new jobs and creating quotes.

Charlie, 31, parent/freelancer

Repetition Tasks can be batch-produced

Repeating tasks

Emails

* Send an email to find out anything important or brand new

* Open and read all emails, including generic ones.

* Reply business emails

* Reply personal emails

Social Media

* Comment on the comments to check business social media accounts

* Write new social media posts

Invoicing

* Invoicing- Create new invoices. Verify payment. Send reminders.

Neue work

* Find freelancing opportunities, apply to new projects

* Update your portfolio and resume with the most recent projects

* Visit job boards and tender board for new projects

It is now time to start putting your new task list in your calendar. There are some concepts that you must first understand before you start to do this.

It's essential to understand when you are most productive.

When are your most productive days?

* Are you quick to get started and do you finish your work quickly?

* Does it take you time to warm up? Do you find that you don't really feel your best until after you've finished your midmorning coffee?

* Is it at the end when everything seems to be coming together and you're doing the best work?

It is vital to identify when you are most alert, awake and ready to accomplish your goals. This requires you to take the time to assess your moods and energy throughout the day. If you aren't sure, keep track of yourself over the next few weeks.

It can be difficult to determine your mood or energy, especially when you look back. Try this simple experiment to determine your mood at end of day. Give yourself a score of 10 for each hour. This will help you to determine your mood, focus, or energy. This will take only 30 seconds and give you valuable insights into hourly productivity.

You can use this information to plan your day in a way which makes sense for you.

Charlie, 31, parent/freelancer

It's essential to understand when you are most productive.

"It is definitely a slow process to get up and running when I start work. I have spent hours getting the kids ready for school and have now completed the first two school runs of the day. I'm ready and waiting for a break. I tend to scroll through my social media feeds or check my emails rather than getting started on work. This adds guilt to my working day.

I was once told that if you spend an hour each morning trying to catch up, you'll lose the rest of your day. That's what I do most days.

With what I know now, it's easier for me to set up a task that is less time-consuming. I'll feel fulfilled when I get something done and keep my plan. However, it is not the right time to start on difficult projects.

Essential skill to master: Understanding your Motives

What motivates your motivation? The most common answer might be:

* A promotion/pay rise

* Provide for your family

* Aiming for early retirement

All these are admirable goals. But, the question here is a little different.

* Do you find it difficult to work on a task that is not your favorite?

* What thoughts do you have?

* What's stopping you taking the easy road and having a vacation or doing something else?

Imagine yourself working on something boring, tedious, or just plain interesting. You're forced to do it but would prefer something else.

It is crucial to understand how to motivate oneself to accomplish difficult tasks. This knowledge can be used to design a productive calendar.

The following statements are very different. Each of the statements can be motivating, while others are completely counter-productive. Do any resonate with your?

I find a way to reward myself after I have completed this task.

Example: I will book a massage for the weekend if I complete this task today. "If I can finish this task by lunchtime I'll go to my favorite cafe for lunch, and I'll save my bagged lunch for tomorrow."

How to use this information. Create a list that lists all the ways you can reward your self for completing tasks. Keep adding to this list as you discover new ways to reward yourself for completing tasks.

Make sure each item is simple, easy to find, and affordable. It would be nice to go to Bali, but it is unlikely you will book one in time to finish your report.

Be sure to keep your word. Get the massage booked, the movie tickets purchased, and then go for lunch.

I'm able to finish this task because it is easier and more rewarding.

Example: "After I finish the report, I will do something simpler like replying emails." "I look forward to scheduling next weeks social media posts. I'll spend the morning doing this more difficult task before moving on to the social media work.

How to use this information It is not a good idea to plan on working for an entire day on a difficult job. To make it easier, set aside a block of time to complete the task. Next, you will need to start a shorter, simpler task. The same schedule can be repeated so you always have something to look forward after a hard day's work.

I can complete this task because someone told me to, and I don't want to feel embarrassed or like I let them down.

Example: I said to everyone that I would complete this by Wednesday. I'd be embarrassed if this deadline is missed. "I told mentors that I was committing myself to this task all day today. They'll think I'm going to have a lot of fun if I don't finish it.

How to use the information: Use external accountability to your advantage if you are motivated by it. To be a mentor, or to share your accountability with, you need to find someone to look up to. Although it might take some time before you find your mentor, or accountability buddy, it will be well worth the effort once you have established a strong relationship.

You are searching to find someone with a unique blend of qualities.

* Experience and knowledge in your area to help them understand your various tasks

* You don't want them to be let down by someone with more seniority or power.

* A genuine interest in you.

Once you've found the right mentor/accountability friend:

* Stay in touch

* Give them your calendar.

* Be honest about how much work you do and the time limits.

* Keep them posted on your progress and deadlines

* Allow them help keep you motivated.

Because there is a strict deadline, I can get through the task.

Example: "This is due within 30 minutes, and it must be done. I can see my boss in the office. They will be following up on any late work. I find it difficult to do anything when I only have a few hours to dedicate to one task. If the same task is due 30 minutes later, I get all fired-up and would do anything to get it done in time.

How to make the most of this information Make up deadlines you can work towards. If you wait two more weeks to get something done, you'll be less motivated. Stick to a shorter deadline.

You can inform the client about the time and assign an accountability buddy to keep you accountable. It's important that the client is available to follow up on any tasks. This will keep you on your toes.

I'm able to complete this task because it is fun.

Example: Yesterday, I submitted $X client work. Today, I will see if I can beat it. "Yesterday I had a productivity rate of 81% at work, and today I'm determined that it will be higher."

How to use the information: What is measured gets improved. The best way to stay motivated is to measure your productivity. This includes measuring:

* Earned money

* Time spent working

* Productivity percentage, minutes worked per hour of total work time.

A simple spreadsheet and graph combination can be used to visual track your progress.

* Keep track of how much money you make each day, if you're a freelancer/have a variable income. You don't want your graph to be ruined by a significant drop in income one day, because you were feeling demotivated.

* You can record the time that you spend studying or working each morning if you are a student, or have a fixed-income salary.

* Note your productivity percentage, if you have defined working hours. Consider, for example, that you have 5 hours (300 mins) of work. You only have 60 minutes per day to do work. Your productivity rate is 20% for the entire day. You can record this data on a chart, and then try to beat it tomorrow. The simple stopwatch app can be used on both your phone and computer to record the time you worked.

Another way to do this is to divide your time into 15-minute increments. You can then measure your output for each section. This method works well when tasks are simple to measure.

If you're working on an assignment or report, for example, this might be the case. You can keep track of the word count each 15 minutes and then calculate how many segments you produced.

This method is not only useful for keeping track of your productivity over time; it also provides another benefit. By measuring every 15 minutes, you can avoid the temptation to do other things for "just few minutes". We all know that the few minutes you spend doing something for a few minutes will end up being a longer time. This will be obvious when you notice that you have written zero words in the past 15 minutes.

I can get through this task because I think of a punishment for myself in case I fail.

Example: "If I don't finish this task by today, then I'm giving my basketball season ticket away." I have $50 cash in an envelope. I have given it my colleague. They want me to mail it to a hate charity unless I can prove that I completed this task.

How to use this information But, the thought of

* Donating money to your least favorite charity

* You give something of value,

* Missing out on an experience that you would have loved

You can keep the fires burning by using this knowledge to your advantage. You must follow through even if you don't accomplish what you set out. If you know the punishment isn't going to happen, then the trick loses its effectiveness.

Your punishment should be planned in advance. Give cash or anything else of value to someone you trust. If you can prove that the task was completed, they'll only return it to you. Choose someone who won't take you in their stride or make excuses for your failure to complete the task. Look for someone who will stand behind you.

Charlie, 31, parent/freelancer

Essential skill to master: Understanding your Motives

"I am motivated through rewards. There were two items on this list that stood out to me. First, I love the rewards I can get myself for completing tasks on time. I enjoy taking the kids out to something after school rather than going straight home. As a reward, I might take the kids to a playground, water park, or restaurant after school.

Second, I feel motivated when I know I have an easier task. This is why I break down more difficult tasks into smaller pieces, such as email work.

Optional Skill to Learn: Estimating Time

Knowing how to accurately estimate how long it will take to accomplish a task is a valuable skill. Time estimates are not required by the calendar system. You will be able to benefit in multiple ways from your time estimation skills.

* If the due date for a task is not given, you can use the ability to estimate how long it will take to help you set a realistic deadline.

* If your job involves quoting for projects, proper time estimating is crucial. Underestimating how long a project will take can lead to you underestimating your own time. If the project takes longer than you expected, you will feel frustrated. Overestimating the time will lead to poor estimates and clients or projects that are lost.

Prioritizing tasks is not an easy task. It is worth considering the time it will take to complete each project. Perhaps you will add a time estimation section to your task listing.

It is a skill. You can improve by repetition and practicing. To improve your time estimation skills, you should start right away if you have difficulty. Make a note of how long you think it will take you to complete any task. Take time to complete the task, and then compare your results.

Most people underestimate the time required to complete tasks. Once you begin to track yourself, you'll be able to identify your tendency.

You can repeat this process as many times as you like. You'll soon notice a greater accuracy in your time estimations.

Blocking Time in Your Calendar

It's time to return to your calendar and start to block in the new tasks you have identified in the previous steps. It's important to remember that we still need to focus on the "Work" block of time. Concentrate only on this area. For now, ignore the rest.

You now have an unbelievable amount of information. You know what times are the most productive for you and which tricks will keep you motivated.

Every Day, Your Last Appointment Is A Review

You should first set aside 15 minutes every day for a review. We'll talk about what happens during your daily overview later. As it stands now, you should make sure that it is in your office for at least the last fifteen minutes of each day.

Schedule Time to Work on Your Task List

Next, determine how much time you'll spend on your task-list. Your bread and butter are the items on your task-list.

* These projects are available to invoice for freelancers or self-employed workers.

* These are the tasks you can do to impress your employer.

These are the assignments you need to complete if your course is a semester-level one.

It is not a good idea to repeat tasks if they don't have an impact on your success. Consider, for example, that you're a freelancer. The task of applying for new projects is a must-do item on your to-do list. It is still a difficult task to apply for new projects. An hour spent actually working on projects for clients is billable. You'll quickly fail as a freelancer if you don't bring in more work. However, you should not spend too much time doing it.

Do not spend more than two thirds of your day on your task lists if you don't know what percentage. You should be able to spend at least two hours per hour on repeating tasks if you have a task list. These time allowances do not include breaks so you cannot expect 100% productivity.

Your calendar will always be in development and you can adjust it as needed.

Now that you know how many hour per day you need to devote to your task list it is time to set this up in your calendar. Use your insights to determine when you are most productive, and what motivates. These insights will help you plan your "tasklist" time.

www.ingramcontent.com/pod-product-compliance
Lightning Source LLC
Chambersburg PA
CBHW071124130526
44590CB00056B/1916